MIDPOINTS

About the Author

Don McBroom (Tucson, AZ) is a Master's Certified Professional Psychological Astrologer with a profound respect for the individual potential represented within every natal chart. In addition to in-person and telephone consultations, he also offers workshops and weekly astrology classes at his office, Personal Astrological Consultations, in Tucson. His Web site, www.donmc.com, features monthly articles with complete archives.

SPECIAL TOPICS IN ASTROLOGY

MIDPOINTS

Identify & Integrate Midpoints
Into Horoscope Synthesis

DON McBROOM

Llewellyn Publications
Woodbury, Minnesota

First Edition
First Printing, 2007

Series design and format by Donna Burch
Cover art © MedioImages/SuperStock
Cover design by Ellen Dahl
Edited by Andrea Neff
Interior illustrations by the Llewellyn Art Department
Llewellyn is a registered trademark of Llewellyn Worldwide, Ltd.

All charts in this book were generated using Win*Star © Matrix Software.

The Library of Congress Cataloging-in-Publication Data
McBroom, Don.
    Midpoints : identify & integrate midpoints into horoscope synthesis / by Don McBroom.—1st ed.
        p. cm.
    Includes bibliographical references and index.
    ISBN: 978-0-7387-0983-3
    1. Horoscopes. I. Title.

BF1728.A2M42 2007
133.5'4—dc22
2007015990

Llewellyn Publications
A Division of Llewellyn Worldwide, Ltd.
2143 Wooddale Drive, Dept. 978-0-7387-0983-3
Woodbury, MN 55125-2989, U.S.A.
www.llewellyn.com

Printed in the United States of America

Other Books in Llewellyn's Special Topics in Astrology Series

Chiron by Martin Lass
(2005)

Vocations by Noel Tyl
(2005)

Eclipses by Celeste Teal
(2006)

Houses by Gwyneth Bryan
(2006)

Aspects by Robin Antepara
(2006)

Aspect Patterns by Stephanie Jean Clement, Ph.D.
(2007)

To the astrologers past, present, and future,
for their relentless pursuit
of a better understanding of human potential

Contents

Figures

Acknowledgments

I would like to gratefully acknowledge and express my sincere appreciation to all those who have made the development of this book a reality.

To Noel Tyl, a modern-day pioneer in psychological astrology, whose techniques, insight, patience, generosity, and encouragement were instrumental in the conception of and creation of this book, I offer my profound heartfelt respect and gratitude.

Thanks to the developers and the technical support staff at Matrix Software—the producers of Win*Star Astrological Software—whose chart forms are used exclusively throughout this book.

Thanks also to Lois Rodden, Mark McDonough, and the entire staff of AstroDatabank™ Software, whose dedicated gathering and compilation of birth data have brought astrological research roaring into the computer age.

To all my students, from whom I have probably learned much more than I have taught, thank you and remember that there is always more to learn.

A special thank you to Laura O'Bagy, for the contribution of her editorial skills and assistance in the development of this book.

Lastly, and most importantly, to my wife, Diana, for her unwavering love, support, and encouragement—thank you.

Foreword

Working with midpoints presents quite a quandary to many: managing a planet or a point tied in by aspect with the middle ground of two or more other planets or points! That's a high level of synthesis, and that's what analytical astrology is all about.

But, astrology is tough enough! Do we need these extra complications? And there are some 858 of them! —"You mean I've got to learn *all* of those descriptions?"

Gratefully, the answer is, "No, you don't!" And Don McBroom proves this to you in this remarkably clear, immediately illuminating textbook.

The first step for us to learn is that midpoint pictures (units of synthesis) are *not* static descriptions; instead, ***midpoint pictures show process***. Think about that for a moment: midpoint pictures are not describing anything that exists; rather, *they are showing what can happen when astrological components get together*. There is a major difference there! Understanding the principle of potentials solves the learning problem. The potential of a nice hearty breakfast is realized through your bringing together bacon and eggs. If you have bacon and eggs together, then you have the potential of a nice hearty breakfast. It's as simple as that!

Therefore, it's not memorization of "this means that when that which means this and this which means that are blended together." Instead, you learn so easily that ***something can be accomplished through the blending of this and that***. Midpoint pictures capture the dynamic common sense of astrological synthesis. You know the symbolisms already; ask yourself, what are their potentials when brought together in different combinations? This book tells you how to think that through…in a flash!

For example, thunder *can be accomplished through* a warm front coming together with a cold front—simple as that! (th = wf/cf)

Creating a child *can be accomplished through* a male merging with a female. (c = m/f)

Those magical words *can be accomplished through* belong to Don McBroom, one of the most patient and skilled teachers and finest writers in astrology today. Believe me, this book is a world-class presentation of a subject that all too easily appears scarily complicated: midpoint synthesis.

And see that equals sign in the equation, in the picture notation? That makes it look off-puttingly scientific and technical, right? But it isn't. The equals sign is simply short-hand for McBroom's action phrase *can be accomplished through*, and it tells us about a strong aspect relationship.

With all my enthusiasm for what Don has accomplished here (I can't stop using that wonderful phrase!), my job is to tell you that this book will enrich your talent, that you will use this book for the rest of your study years in astrology. This book will ignite your thinking process so easily, and it will never cool down!

What do midpoints do for horoscope analysis?

When we realize that every planet in the horoscope is actually in dynamic relationship with every other planet—putting our organizational use of orbs aside—we get the sense of the wholeness of personality. Every part is somehow going to reflect the identity of that whole. And our use of midpointology, to coin a phrase, approaches that wholeness, adds to it, and brings us further toward the individual's reality.

A vast majority of the midpoint pictures our computer gives us will echo what we glean from our analytical preparation of the horoscope proper. BUT, in every horoscope, several pictures will ADD dramatically to that initial preparation. These are dynamic glimpses of synthesis that suggest much about the individual that we may not have suspected. In my years of analytical work with astrology, I have seen many, many cases brought individualistically to life, punctuated by a pivotal, keenly wrought midpoint picture. For example, a midpoint group picture for strong depression easily hidden by a super-happy behavioral profile on display for all to see. Or the aggressive ego-drive cloaked by a mantle of introversion.

Midpoint pictures do wonders for harnessing "unaspected" planets. Just what are you going to do with Napoleon's peregrine SUN? There is a very telling midpoint picture here that helps us: Sun = Mercury/Neptune. Suddenly the Sun is brought into the planetary mix, brought into the fold, so to speak: identity definition and ego needs (☉) *can be accomplished through* thinking and communicating (☿) imaginatively (♆), formulating strategy, to fit Napoleon's reality!

And what about Muhammad Ali's ☉ = ♃/☊? Ego definition (☉) *can be accomplished through* exuberant and effusive (♃) public presentation (☊)! Remember his trademark statement, "I am (☉) the greatest (♃)?"

You see! You've already become comfortable with the process!

McBroom even shows how *the closest* midpoint picture gains a particularly loud voice in synthesis. And his patient teaching readies you before you know it for an easy sophistication with indirect midpoints used in the predictive system of solar arcs!

All those famous people!

McBroom works with hundreds and hundreds of midpoint measurements of famous people. It is simply fascinating to see Napoleon's ☉ = ☿/♆ imaginative-strategy picture shared by Grandma Moses and Wolfgang Amadeus Mozart! All three of these famous people defined themselves—*achieved their identity* (☉)—through the use of their imaginative and artistic (♆) communication (☿). And would you believe Muppets creator Jim Henson and the Marquis de Sade as well!

McBroom brings television evangelist Jim Bakker's closest midpoint picture forward: ☉ = ♂/Asc, suggesting that his career pursuits and public status (Mc) *can be accomplished through* energetic (♂) self-promotion (♂/Asc).

Then we see evangelist Billy Graham's closest midpoint picture (precisely exact) to be Mc = ☽/♇. This suggests that Graham's public image and his career pursuits *can be accomplished through* dealing with emotional needs within an empowerment perspective, toward some kind of transformation.

See how it works!

Don McBroom brings midpointology to celebrity status. His writing is simply brilliant and his "teacher touch" is gentle. He is the midpoint between the astrologer and specially measured knowledge.

Think what YOU *can accomplish* with this dynamite know-how!

Thank you, Don McBroom, for one of the finest astrology texts I have ever read.

Noel Tyl
Fountain Hills, AZ
August 2005

Preface

Several conventions have been established for the organization of this book. I have adopted these considerations in an attempt to make the presentation of the material as concise as possible.

For example, rather than using the cumbersome phrases "his or her" and "he or she," I have chosen to use, for simplicity and readability, the masculine forms, unless a particular female is being discussed. My choice is based on total respect for both genders and with full intention that any specific reference would be equally appropriate for either males or females.

Famous people and other well-known public individuals are used as examples extensively throughout this book, with a minimum of biographical descriptions presented. I have attempted to use individuals who are well-known, thus allowing more attention to be focused on the application of the interpretive techniques rather than on lengthy biographies or case histories.

Every effort has been made to use the most accurate birth data available. Birth data throughout this book have been obtained from AstroDatabank™ software. This software provides a database of birth information collected and compiled by Lois Rodden, Mark McDonough, and the AstroDatabank staff. Rodden Ratings[1] rank the reliability of the individual birth information. AA, A, and B data are most commonly used in this text. In cases where the birth time is unknown, this fact is called to the reader's attention. In these cases—based on the specific planets involved—the measurements referred to are appropriate regardless of the birth time.

References to a particular individual may be found in multiple locations throughout this book. While this may seem initially counterintuitive, I made the decision to insert the references into the location that was most appropriate to the specific astrological discussion rather than grouping all references to a particular individual in a single place. By utilizing this format, the continuity of a particular discussion could be reasonably maintained. All references to specific individuals can be found in the index.

Individual listings within a particular discussion are grouped together *only* by virtue of similar astrological measurements. Again, these listings are presented in no particular order, with only the appropriateness of the astrological measurement being considered. No relative or hierarchical comparison of the intensity of any measurement for a particular individual within any list is implied or intended.

Astrology no longer views measurements as being symbolic of unalterable, predestined outcomes. This concept is kept in mind throughout this book. Delineated interpretations of specific midpoint pictures often include the word *suggests* to reinforce the importance of free will and latitude of personal expression when evaluating any specific measurement.

Suggested interpretations are as inclusive as possible while maintaining a manageable size. The initial suggestion of a midpoint picture's influence will be further embellished with additional layers of interpretation that fit in with the measurement. While many of these secondary levels of interpretation could not have been reasonably anticipated in advance, they are nonetheless instructive and reinforce the individuality with which one utilizes the particular measurement's influence.

When deemed appropriate and instructive, I have noted parenthetically within the text immediately following the associated word specific planetary references within interpretations. For example, an interpretation might include "communication (☿)," indicating that the word *communication* is frequently associated with the planet Mercury.

Whenever possible, specific techniques not previously discussed will be reserved for inclusion in the most appropriate sequence to provide the maximum continuity of the presentation.

All charts were calculated using the Placidus house system. References to the North Node refer to the Mean Node position.

---

1. **Accuracy and Rodden Ratings:** *AA, A, and B data are the only data that should be used in astrological studies.* Data rated "AA" (from birth certificate or birth record) are the most accurate obtainable. Data rated "A" (from memory) are usually accurate, but there are exceptions. Politicians and entertainers are notorious for giving misleading birth dates and times, except when consulting their astrologer. "B" data (from biographies) are similarly accurate, because authors who give times are likely to have obtained the data from the subject, the subject's immediate family, or a birth record.

Introduction

Why Use Midpoints?

As you begin your study of midpoints, you may be overwhelmed and intimidated by long lists of seemingly indecipherable planetary relationships. You may wonder, "Will the results be worth my efforts?" Let me offer some words of encouragement.

Rewarding results from midpoint analysis can come surprisingly quickly and easily. Rather than having to learn a whole new set of complicated rules, you can simply add to the information you have already learned. It is a matter of adding detail, nuance, depth, and specificity as opposed to starting from scratch. By using the cumulative knowledge already at your disposal, you can quickly begin to use midpoints to gain access to a deeper interpretive meaning. One of my advanced students recently described her first experience with midpoints. While she admitted feeling overwhelmed initially, she related it this way:

> I'd compare midpoint analysis to watching a movie on a DVD and then finding that the menu included an "extra features" option. Previously unknown details were revealed that opened up a way to better understand the story line. The extra features presented information about the major performers and their interrelationships, scenes that were cut, and alternate endings. Details that had seemed vague

were suddenly brought into focus. These newly discovered details enhanced my understanding of the story line and made the overall experience that much more fulfilling.

This analogy applies to midpoints. Had I not decided to explore midpoints (i.e., the extra features), I would have missed the details that truly make up the whole picture.

If you haven't yet experienced the subtle yet dramatic power of midpoints, those same discoveries await you. Regardless of your level of astrological experience, if you have a firm grasp of the basic planets, signs, houses, and aspects, you're ready to embark on the pursuit of midpoints.

While midpoints share some similarities with planetary *aspects*, midpoints typically reveal even more intricate relationships between the planets, further blending and melding their collective meanings together. These multilayered relationships evolve and grow as new interconnections become apparent. Midpoint analysis takes us beyond the tip of the iceberg to reveal additional information that previously had been concealed beneath the surface.

Using midpoints can be distilled to three steps:

1. Identification and organization

2. Interpretation and analysis

3. Integration and synthesis

As you progress through this book, I'm confident that midpoints will prove both accessible and profound, and that the powerful insight they can provide will encourage you to include midpoints as a permanent part of your astrological repertoire.

CHAPTER ONE

Midpoint Identification and Organization

In nature we never see anything isolated,
but everything in connection with something else
which is before it, beside it, under it and over it.

—GÖETHE

Midpoint Definitions and Terminology

As with astrological aspects, midpoints also represent a way to connect separate individual components within the horoscope. Using aspects and midpoints allows us to combine and merge these diverse influences into tangible expressions—and interpretive impressions—that are profoundly useful in the analysis of the horoscope.

However, instead of the **two** planets or points involved with an *aspect* relationship, there are **three** distinct components represented by each *midpoint picture*. Because midpoints represent more combinations than can be efficiently integrated into an aspect grid, a different way is required to express and concisely describe these three-way interactions.

For example, let's assume that the Sun is exactly in between (at the *midpoint* of) Mercury and Neptune. This midpoint relationship is expressed in equation form as:

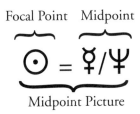

However, before we go further, it is important to have a firm understanding of midpoint terminology. In the example above, the Sun is referred to as the **Focal Point**,[1] Mercury/Neptune is the **midpoint**, and the whole equation is called the **midpoint picture**.

The Focal Point occupies a position halfway between the two planets or points on the right side of the equation, and the midpoint picture may be expressed verbally as "the Sun is at the midpoint of Mercury and Neptune" or, even more simply, "Sun equals Mercury/Neptune" ("Sun equals Mercury Neptune").

Convention has determined that the right-hand side of the equation is expressed by listing the faster-moving planet first (e.g., ☉ = ☿/♆ rather than ☉ = ♆/☿).[2]

The midpoint picture describes in astrological shorthand how the Focal Point connects with, is merged with, and is colored by the meanings of the other two planets or points.

Identification of Midpoint Pictures

Although it may be tempting to include Chiron and asteroids and everything else in the midpoint analysis, I strongly suggest that (at least initially) you include only the planets,[3] the North Node, the Ascendant, and the Midheaven until you become familiar with midpoint concepts.

Some midpoint pictures can be seen relatively easily just by visual inspection of the natal chart. For example, in Jim Henson's natal chart (figure 1) we see that the Sun is approximately midway between (i.e., at the midpoint of) Mercury and Neptune. The Sun is roughly 13° away from Mercury (14♎ minus 01♎ equals 13°) and 14° away from Neptune (an additional 13° takes Neptune from 17♍ to 00♎, plus the 1° to get to 01♎ for a total of 14°). This describes a midpoint picture that is expressed as "Sun equals Mercury/Neptune" and is written in the astrological equation:

$$\odot = \mercury/\neptune$$

Unfortunately, not all midpoint pictures are this easily identified. For a complete and thorough analysis, a computer is invaluable.

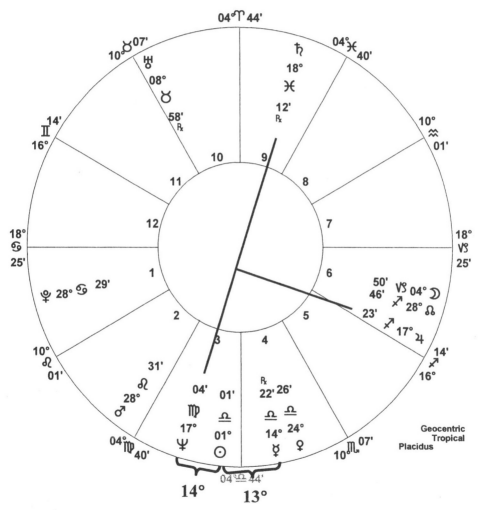

Figure 1. Jim Henson's Natal Chart Showing ☉ = ☿/♆ and a Saturn-Neptune-Jupiter T-Square

Jim Henson
September 24, 1936 / Greenville, MS / 12:10 AM CST
Placidus Houses

The 90° Midpoint Sort

Why Use a 90° Sort?

Tension, particularly as suggested by conjunctions, squares, and oppositions, is a vital component of the horoscope—and of life itself. Without tension, there is really no motivation to change, grow, or evolve. Without tension, we might well be content just to *exist*. But tension makes us uncomfortable enough that we're motivated to *do something*. Midpoints that illustrate this tension have a pronounced potential impact on both the chart interpretation and the client's life.

The 90° Midpoint Sort visually compresses the entire 360° of the horoscope into just 90°. By doing so, all cardinal, all fixed, and all mutable signs are grouped together and arranged as if they were stacked or layered upon all other signs and degrees of the same *mode* (figure 2).

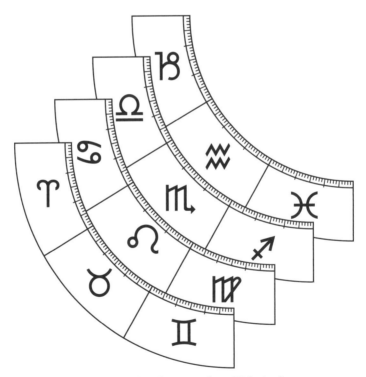

Figure 2. Visual Explanation of 90° Midpoint Sort

Jim Henson ***Sep 24, 1936*** ***12:10:00 AM CST*** ***091W03'00"*** ***33N24'00"***

Midpoint Sort: 90° Dial											
☿/♆	000°43'	☉/♀	012°44'	♂/☊	028°39'	☊/Mc	046°45'	☉/♇	059°45'	♄	078°12'
☉	001°01'	♅/♆	013°01'	☽/♂	031°41'	♆/Asc	047°44'	☿/Asc	061°23'	♅/♇	078°44'
☿/♄	001°17'	♄/♅	013°35'	♀/♅	031°42'	☽/☉	047°55'	♇/Mc	061°37'	☿/♂	081°27'
☽/☊	001°48'	♇/☊	013°38'	♃/♆	032°13'	♄/Asc	048°18'	♅/☊	063°52'	♃/☊	083°05'
☉/Mc	002°52'	☿	014°22'	♃/♄	032°48'	☽/Mc	049°47'	♀/Asc	066°26'	☉/♆	084°02'
♃/Asc	002°54'	♀/Mc	014°35'	♆/☊	037°55'	♀/♃	050°55'	☿/♇	066°26'	☉/♄	084°36'
♂/♅	003°45'	☽/♇	016°40'	♂/Asc	038°28'	☿/☊	051°34'	☽/♅	066°54'	♆/Mc	085°54'
Mc	004°44'	Asc	018°25'	♄/☊	038°29'	♆/♇	052°46'	♂/♆	067°47'	☽/♃	086°07'
☽	004°50'	☿/♀	019°24'	♅	038°58'	♄/♇	053°21'	♂/♄	068°22'	♄/Mc	086°28'
♀/♆	005°45'	☉/♅	019°59'	☉/♃	039°12'	☽/☿	054°36'	♀/♇	071°28'	♀/♂	086°29'
♀/♄	006°19'	♅/Mc	021°51'	☽/♆	040°57'	☉/Asc	054°43'	♅/Asc	073°41'	☊	088°46'
☉/☿	007°41'	♂/♃	022°57'	♃/Mc	041°04'	Mc/Asc	056°35'	☉/♂	074°46'		
♃/♇	007°56'	♇/Asc	023°27'	☽/♄	041°31'	♀/☊	056°36'	♂/Mc	076°38'		
☊/Asc	008°35'	♀	024°26'	♂/♇	043°30'	♃/♅	058°11'	♆	077°04'		
☿/Mc	009°33'	☿/♅	026°40'	☉/☊	044°53'	♂	058°31'	♃	077°23'		
☽/Asc	011°37'	♇	028°29'	☿/♃	045°53'	☽/♀	059°38'	♄/♆	077°38'		

00°00'–29°59' = Cardinal Sign Placement (♈ ♋ ♎ ♑)
30°00'–59°59' = Fixed Sign Placement (♉ ♌ ♏ ♒)
60°00'–89°59' = Mutable Sign Placement (♊ ♍ ♐ ♓)

Figure 3. 90° Midpoint Sort

This 90° Midpoint Sort (figure 3) is particularly helpful by virtue of the fact that it groups together planets and midpoints that are **conjunct**, **square**, or **in opposition** to one another. Their close proximity in the list highlights and emphasizes the *tension* between these points and adds to the significance of the resultant midpoint pictures.

As we analyze individual midpoint pictures, it isn't necessary to differentiate between these specific types of challenging aspects. Whether it's a conjunction, a square, or an opposition, for midpoint purposes they're all equal—equally capable of producing *tension*; **hence, the *equals sign* in the equation that describes the midpoint picture**.

Many astrology software programs[4] produce 90° Midpoint Sorts that contain ninety-one individual listings including the ten planets, the North Node, the Ascendant, the Midheaven, and the seventy-eight specific midpoint positions between these planets and points. This initial list may seem somewhat daunting just due to the sheer quantity of information it represents.

Fortunately, it isn't necessary—or even desirable—to examine all possible individual midpoints. Midpoint analysis is a powerful tool, but we need to be able to separate the astrological wheat from the chaff. As we progress, we'll narrow down our list to a much more reasonable size. Our first logical step is to spend some time considering *orbs*.

Orbs

Midpoint relationships need not be *exact* to merit our consideration. But practically, we do need to establish some working guidelines to make the scope of our analysis more manageable.

As with *aspects*, the closer a midpoint measurement is to being exact (i.e., within a tighter *orb*), the more weight and credence are given that particular measurement and its corresponding interpretation. Conversely, the further away a measurement is from being exact, the less likely it is to have any meaningful importance in our analysis. It is practical to consider only midpoint pictures within a 2°–2.5° orb[5] of a particular planet or point.[6]

As discussed previously, while the 90° Midpoint Sort has ninety-one individual listings, it represents a variable number of actual *midpoint pictures* with the final number determined by the number of midpoints that are located within the orb of each of the Focal Points.

In our example in figure 4 (Jim Henson's 90° Midpoint Sort), the last five midpoints listed in the first column are not within the defined 2° orb of any Focal Point. These and other midpoints beyond the 2° orb have a solid line through them. These particular midpoints aren't close enough to any Focal Point to merit any further consideration.

As we look in more detail at Jim Henson's 90° Midpoint Sort, it is also important to note that sometimes more than one Focal Point can share a single midpoint. To illustrate this, the three planets shown in Henson's natal T-Square in figure 1 (Saturn, Neptune, and Jupiter) are all located in the 77°–79° range of the 90° Midpoint Sort shown in figure 4.

Jim Henson Sep 24, 1936 12:10:00 AM CST 091W03'00" 33N24'0Q"

Midpoint Sort: 90° Dial

☿/♆	000°43'	☉/♀	012°44'	♂/☊	028°39'	~~☊/Mc~~	~~046°45'~~	☉/♇	059°45'	♄	078°12'
☉	001°01'	♅/♆	013°01'	~~☽/♂~~	~~031°41'~~	~~♆/Asc~~	~~047°44'~~	~~☿/Asc~~	~~061°23'~~	♅/♇	078°44'
☿/♄	001°17'	♄/♅	013°35'	~~♀/♅~~	~~031°42'~~	~~☽/☉~~	~~047°55'~~	~~♇/Mc~~	~~061°37'~~	~~☿/♂~~	~~081°27'~~
☽/☊	001°48'	♇/☊	013°38'	~~♃/♆~~	~~032°13'~~	~~♄/Asc~~	~~048°18'~~	~~♅/☊~~	~~063°52'~~	~~♃/☊~~	~~083°05'~~
☉/Mc	002°52'	☿	014°22'	~~♃/♄~~	~~032°48'~~	~~☽/Mc~~	~~049°47'~~	~~♀/Asc~~	~~066°26'~~	~~☉/♆~~	~~084°02'~~
♃/Asc	002°54'	♀/Mc	014°35'	♆/☊	037°55'	~~♀/♃~~	~~050°55'~~	~~☿/♇~~	~~066°26'~~	~~☉/♄~~	~~084°36'~~
♂/♅	003°45'	☽/♇	016°40'	♂/Asc	038°28'	~~☿/☊~~	~~051°34'~~	~~☽/♅~~	~~066°54'~~	~~♆/Mc~~	~~085°54'~~
Mc	004°44'	Asc	018°25'	♄/☊	038°29'	~~♆/♇~~	~~052°46'~~	~~♂/♆~~	~~067°47'~~	~~☽/♃~~	~~086°07'~~
☽	004°50'	☿/♀	019°24'	♅	038°58'	~~♄/♇~~	~~053°21'~~	~~♂/♄~~	~~068°22'~~	~~♄/Mc~~	~~086°28'~~
♀/♆	005°45'	☉/♅	019°59'	☉/♃	039°12'	~~☽/☿~~	~~054°36'~~	~~♀/♇~~	~~071°28'~~	~~♀/♂~~	~~086°29'~~
♀/♄	006°19'	~~♅/Mc~~	~~021°51'~~	☽/♆	040°57'	~~☉/Asc~~	~~054°43'~~	~~♅/Asc~~	~~073°41'~~	☊	088°46'
~~☉/☿~~	~~007°41'~~	♂/♃	022°57'	~~♃/Mc~~	~~041°04'~~	Mc/Asc	056°35'	~~☉/♂~~	~~074°46'~~		
~~♃/♇~~	~~007°56'~~	♇/Asc	023°27'	~~☽/♄~~	~~041°31'~~	♀/☊	056°36'	♂/Mc	076°38'		
~~☊/Asc~~	~~008°35'~~	♀	024°26'	~~♂/♇~~	~~043°30'~~	♃/♅	058°11'	♆	077°04'		
~~☿/Mc~~	~~009°33'~~	☿/♅	026°40'	~~☉/☊~~	~~044°53'~~	♂	058°31'	♃	077°23'		
~~☽/Asc~~	~~011°37'~~	♇	028°29'	~~☿/♃~~	~~045°53'~~	☽/♀	059°38'	♄/♆	077°38'		

Figure 4. Jim Henson's 90° Midpoint Sort

In this compressed 90° format, these positions equate to the 17°–19° range of their corresponding *mutable* natal sign positions. For these three planets, then, we are looking for midpoints grouped within a plus or minus 2° orb of each planet:

For Neptune at 77°04' we look for midpoints between 75°04 and 79°04'.

For Jupiter at 77°23' we look for midpoints between 75°23' and 79°23'.

For Saturn at 78°12' we look for midpoints between 76°12' and 80°12'.

We see that three specific midpoints are in close proximity and fall within the 2° orb of each of these planets:

♂/Mc at 76°38'

♄/♆ at 77°38'

♅/♇ at 78°44'

Because all three planets share these common midpoints, we can compile the following midpoint pictures:

♆ = ♂/Mc

♃ = ♂/Mc

$\hbar = \sigma'/Mc$

$4 = \hbar/\Psi$

$\Psi = \aleph/\Psi$

$4 = \aleph/\Psi$

$\hbar = \aleph/\Psi$

Note: We exclude as meaningless any potential midpoint picture in which the same planet or point is on both sides of the equation (e.g., $\hbar = \hbar/\Psi$ and $\Psi = \hbar/\Psi$).

An additional word of clarification is needed as we look at this 90° Midpoint Sort. With the North Node at 88°46', we are looking for midpoints between 86°46' and 90°46'. Because the 90° Midpoint Sort appropriately ends at 90°, we must loop back to the first column to include any midpoints up to 00°46' on this form. Therefore, the Mercury/Neptune midpoint at 00°43' on the list is still within the established 2° orb of the North Node and gives us the midpoint picture $\Omega = \yen/\Psi$.

As shown in figure 5, we're left with forty-three valid midpoint pictures for Jim Henson that are within a 2° orb. That's still quite a lot of data. We'll narrow it down further a little later, but first let's explore a slightly different way to display midpoint pictures.

90° Midpoint Pictures—Jim Henson

☉ = ☿/Ψ	☿ = ♅/Ψ	♂ = Mc/Asc
☉ = ☿/♄	☿ = ♄/♅	♂ = ♀/☊
☉ = ☽/☊	☿ = Ψ/☊	♂ = ♃/♅
☉ = ☉/Mc**	☿ = ♀/Mc	♂ = ☽/♀
☉ = ♃/Asc	Asc = ☽/Ψ	♂ = ☉/♇
Mc = ☉/Mc**	Asc = ☿/♀	Ψ = ♂/Mc
Mc = ♃/Asc	Asc = ☉/♅	Ψ = ♄/Ψ**
Mc = ♂/♅	♀ = ♂/♃	Ψ = ♅/♇
Mc = ♀/Ψ	♀ = ♇/Asc	♃ = ♂/Mc
Mc = ♀/♄	♇ = ☿/♅	♃ = ♄/Ψ
☽ = ☉/Mc	♇ = ♂/☊	♃ = ♅/♇
☽ = ♃/Asc	♅ = Ψ/☊	♄ = ♂/Mc
☽ = ♂/♅	♅ = ♂/Asc	♄ = ♄/Ψ**
☽ = ♀/Ψ	♅ = ♄/☊	♄ = ♅/♇
☽ = ♀/♄	♅ = ☉/♃	☊ = ☿/Ψ
☿ = ☉/♀	♅ = ☽/Ψ	

** **Note:** We exclude as meaningless any potential Midpoint Picture in which the same planet or point is on both sides of the equation (e.g., ☉ = ☉/Mc, Mc = ☉/Mc, Ψ = ♄/Ψ, and ♄ = ♄/Ψ).

Figure 5. Jim Henson's Midpoint Pictures Using a 2° Orb

The 90° Midpoint Tree

An alternate way to show the 90° midpoint information is to use the 90° Midpoint *Tree* (figure 6). Both the 90° Midpoint Sort and the 90° Midpoint Tree can be used to identify midpoint pictures that are within orb of any particular Focal Point.

The 90° Midpoint Tree is different in that the information is grouped together by each Focal Point and then sorted by midpoint within the closest orb of each Focal Point. The same midpoint pictures are identified with both the 90° Midpoint Sort and the 90° Midpoint Tree formats.

090°00' MIDPOINT TREES FOR JIM HENSON
Orb Allowed: 02°00'   Sorted by Closest Orb

☽		Orb
♀ — ♆		+00°55'
♅ — ♂	D	-01°05'
♀ — ♄	D	+01°29'
Asc — ♃		-01°56'
Mc — ☉	D	-01°58'

☉		Orb
☿ — ♄		+00°16'
☿ — ♆	D	-00°18'
☽ — ☊		+00°47'
Asc — ♃	D	+01°53'

☿		Orb
♀ — Mc		+00°13'
♀ — ☊	D	-00°44'
♅ — ♄	D	-00°47'
♅ — ♆		-01°21'
♀ — ☉	D	-01°38'

♀		Orb
♇ — Asc		-00°59'
♂ — ♃	D	-01°29'

♂

♂		Orb
♃ — ♅	D	-00°20'
☽ — ♀		+01°07'
☉ — ♇	D	+01°14'
☊ — ♀		-01°55'
Mc — Asc		-01°56'

♃		Orb
♄ — ♆	D	+00°15'
Mc — ♂	D	-00°45'
♇ — ♅	D	+01°21'

♄		Orb
♇ — ♅		+00°32'
Mc — ♂		-01°34'

♅		Orb
♃ — ☉	D	+00°14'
♄ — ☊		-00°29'
♂ — Asc		-00°30'
♆ — ☊	D	-01°03'
♆ — ☽	D	+01°59'

☿

♆		Orb
Mc — ♂		-00°26'
♇ — ♅		+01°40'

♇		Orb
♂ — ☊		+00°10'
♅ — ☿	D	-01°49'

☊		Orb
☿ — ♆		-01°57'

Mc		Orb
♅ — ♂		-00°59'
♀ — ♆	D	+01°01'
♀ — ♄		+01°35'
Asc — ♃	D	-01°50'

As		Orb
♀ — ☿		+00°59'
♅ — ☉	D	+01°34'
♇ — ☽		-01°45'

Figure 6. Jim Henson's 90° Midpoint Tree

While the 90° Midpoint Tree may arguably provide a more straightforward method of identifying midpoint pictures, some sacrifices must be made when using this format by itself, specifically:

- Midpoints may not be listed in the standard order of fastest to slowest speed.

- We cannot locate the very important Sun/Moon or Ascendant/Midheaven midpoints unless they are within orb of a Focal Point.

- We cannot identify midpoint pictures within orb of the Aries Point (which will be discussed in detail in chapter 3).

Personally, I prefer to use both forms, thereby utilizing the strengths of each. For a more detailed comparison of the 90° Midpoint Sort and the 90° Midpoint Tree, please refer to appendix I.

---

1. In this book, the planet or point to the left of the equals sign is referred to as the *Focal Point*.

2. The single exception to this rule is that the Sun/Moon midpoint is routinely listed as ☉/☽ even though the Moon moves faster from a geocentric perspective.

3. Includes the Sun and the Moon as planets, even though technically they are luminaries.

4. Including Matrix Software's *Win*Star 90° Midpoint Tyl* chart form that is used in this book.

5. A 2° orb is used in this book except where specifically noted otherwise.

6. A *point* refers to the Ascendant, Midheaven, North Node, or any other nonplanetary position.

CHAPTER TWO

Midpoint Interpretation and Analysis

Develop your senses—especially learn how to see.
Realise that everything connects to everything else.

—LEONARDO DA VINCI

Utilization of Keywords in Midpoint Analysis

When each of us began our individual study of astrology, the process was quite similar to learning a new language. And really, that's exactly what astrology is—a symbolic language utilizing some rather foreign-looking glyphs.

The astrological glyphs represent a shorthand method that is used to trigger specific astrological associations in our brains. Early on, it is important that we develop and build a strong vocabulary of *nontechnical* keywords associated with each of the glyphs. By doing so, it is easier to assemble any particular measurement into an intelligible, meaningful, descriptive sentence. Moreover, this process reinforces our ability to clearly comprehend and relate practical interpretations without the astrological jargon that can easily cloud rather than clarify the message.

As we begin to understand the symbolic interpretive meanings of a specific planet, our initial impressions eventually are colored and enhanced by the sign placement, and still further refined and modified by the planet's house placement. It quickly becomes obvious that we need a clear and concise way of managing and processing these increasingly complex meanings.

When *aspects* are introduced, the plot really thickens. We continue to figuratively build upon the basic skeleton of the horoscope as we add successive layers of symbolic nerves, muscles, and connective tissue. Gradually an impression of the complete individual begins to emerge, rather than just a grocery list of unconnected bits and pieces. And while each measurement has its own merits, a much more useful and specific interpretation is possible when we are able to integrate these seemingly disparate components. Without this integration, the numerous fragments of individual measurements can lead us toward confusion rather than enlightenment.

We work toward constructing a coherent, intelligible, and integrated synthesis of the chart. The resultant impressions and suggestions allow us to compile a working idea of how specific motivations combine to form a unique individual—his needs, strengths, talents, challenges, fears, and, perhaps most importantly, *potential*.

Once we can do this easily and fluidly, our core understanding improves and we are better able to grasp and integrate meanings. The technical measurements themselves become less elusive and less important—and simultaneously and paradoxically gain real significance as we solidify their interpretive meanings.

You are encouraged to use any keywords that resonate with you. The interpretive meanings presented in this book are based on the keywords that I've become most comfortable with and are intended to serve only as examples as you formulate your own individual interpretations.

The Importance of Polarities

By nature we have no defect that could not become a strength,
no strength that could not become a defect.
—GÖETHE

Early on in our studies we may have been tempted to look at any given measurement as either "good" or "bad." Many of the old texts left little interpretive room for individual responses to astrological influences and were often dismally depressing. If we are doomed to a predestined, preordained fate, then what is the point of living?

As the practice of astrology has evolved, so has our respect for and appreciation of the importance of free will in our lives. Free will is accompanied by the recognition that our conscious choices and multiple other factors determine our ultimate destinies. We're no longer stubbornly and helplessly locked into the belief that challenging measurements always portend unavoidable doom. Neither should we blindly trust that even a preponderance of easy aspects would magically absolve us from any personal responsibility for what ultimately happens to us.

Our job as astrologers is to provide the client with objective and practical information that can enhance self-understanding, improve the quality of decision making, and provide some direction in the pursuit of a specific path of his choosing. This is a pretty tall order to fill, given that we frequently find ourselves evaluating a horoscope with multiple difficult or challenging measurements. It may be the placement of a specific planet by sign, house, aspect, or other measurement that, when considered by itself, seems to have the potential to be particularly problematic. Although presenting the information to the client in an objective and direct way is rarely easy, it is without question both desirable and necessary.

Every possible astrological influence has a relatively wide range of potential expectations, from the least positive to the most positive. For example, Saturn has long had a reputation for being the unwelcome wet blanket on our picnic or a frustrating roadblock on our path to success. But Saturn isn't just about rules, restrictions, repression, delays, and frustration. Saturn has a positive side as well, signifying structure, a solid foundation, ambition, discipline, and necessary controls. Ultimately, we must choose how Saturn's influence is to be used—for better or worse.

As we proceed with our midpoint study, it is vitally important to keep in mind the *polarities* of probable responses. By embracing this concept, we can better understand that although our birth charts will never change, *our response to the individual influences suggested in our horoscope is not necessarily static and can indeed be modified to benefit us.* A challenging or even a potentially debilitating influence can feasibly be turned into a powerful asset. Conversely, an easy or supportive measurement can result in more meaningful gains when we work with it rather than sitting idly by, waiting for all those wonderful goodies to magically fall into our laps.

Only when we become aware of these anticipated extremes of behavior can we begin to grasp the real power of astrology and begin to transform both ourselves and the lives of our clients. We can then set our sights on something approaching our highest potential rather than passively gravitating toward the less productive and less rewarding extremes.

Interpreting Midpoints

Now that the necessary foundation has been laid, we can begin to construct interpretive meanings from individual midpoint pictures. The combinations of *keywords, polarities,* and the *anticipated ranges of expression* can now be used to interpret and summarize any given midpoint picture. Our goal is to connect the individual components of the midpoint picture in a consistent and logical way as we formulate the analytical interpretation.

Using the following simple sentence format, we can plug in keywords associated with each planet or point—substituting the equals sign with the phrase "can be accomplished through"—as we construct a descriptive, interpretive sentence. Suggested keywords are provided in appendix II.

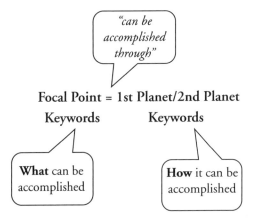

To demonstrate this technique, we will use some examples from Jim Henson's 90° Midpoint Sort (figure 4) and Midpoint Tree (figure 6).

$\odot = \math$ ☽/♌   *Life purpose and ego definition (☉) can be accomplished through emotionally relating (☽) to others or to the public (♌).*

♂ = ☽/♀   *Efficient use of energy (♂) can be accomplished through emotionally relating (☽) by using social or artistic pursuits (♀).*

♅ = ☽/♆   *Individualistic expression and innovation (♅) can be accomplished through emotionally relating (☽) by using idealism, imagination, or fantasy (♆).*

Asc = ☽/♇   *Identity definition and identity projection (Asc) can be accomplished through intensely (♇) emotionally relating (☽), or through an emotional (☽) empowerment leading to a change in perspective and transformation (♇).*

It becomes apparent that the interpretations of all four of these midpoint pictures share the common phrase "emotionally relating." The use of this common phrasing reinforces the fact that we don't have to memorize pages and pages of interpretations, but rather that we only need a good grasp of the keywords associated with each of the planets or points. In this example, we can see that the common thread is the involvement of the Moon on the right-hand side of our midpoint picture. With very little practice, you will find that the interpretive meanings are easy to formulate and express.

The specific wording of the interpretation should incorporate keywords for all the elements of the midpoint picture, but the exact phrases need not be strictly adhered to. It is most important to formulate an understandable concept that summarizes the suggestion made by the midpoint picture.

Examples of Polarities in Midpoint Analysis

With midpoints—as with any astrological measurement—it is important not to assume that any specific manifestations or outcomes are automatic and guaranteed. Let me offer some examples of midpoint interpretation to demonstrate this point.

Referring back to the chart for Jim Henson (page 5, figure 1), we see that one of the midpoint pictures represented is ☉ = ☿/♆.

Using keywords to construct an interpretation, we arrive at something like this:

Life purpose and ego definition (☉) can be accomplished through thoughts and ideas (☿) that are communicated (☿) imaginatively or by using fantasy (♆).

So would we logically expect that anyone and everyone with this particular midpoint picture would become a professional puppeteer and inventor of the Muppets? Of course not. But it is interesting and instructive to see some other high-profile people who share this very same midpoint picture and for whom the interpretation is no less appropriate.

- Amazingly, Walt Disney also has ☉ = ☿/♆. Although he didn't invent the Muppets, he did develop numerous fantasy (♆) cartoon characters and spent his lifetime (☉) communicating (☿) through them by using *movies and film* (both of which are related to Neptune).

- With the anticipated imaginative communication helping to define life purpose, it isn't a big surprise to find that inventor Thomas Edison[1] shares the ☉ = ☿/♆ midpoint as well. Isn't it amazing that when a cartoon character experiences a thoughtful (☿) inspiration (♆), the cartoonist symbolizes the moment by a *light bulb* being illuminated over the character's head! If it weren't for Edison's historic invention, that symbolism couldn't possibly exist. Also, when considering that Neptune also relates to movies and film, recall that Edison invented motion (☿) pictures (♆), which, not incidentally, required that light (☉) be projected through the film (♆) for the effect to be accomplished. Further, remember that motion pictures are actually multiple sequences of still images that create the illusion (♆) of movement (☿).

- Because spirituality is also a Neptune-related keyword, we might anticipate someone who communicates (☿) spiritual (♆) concepts as part of the manifestation of his life purpose (☉) to have the ☉ = ☿/♆ midpoint picture. Does the physician/author Deepak Chopra fit the description? He certainly does.

- Former Beatle John Lennon also shares the same ☉ = ☿/♆ midpoint with Jim Henson. Isn't it interesting to recall that one of Lennon's most popular songs was "Imagine"? Lennon says in his lyrics, "You may say (☿) I'm (☉) a dreamer (♆)..." To reinforce this theme, Lennon also has Asc = ♃/♆—identity definition and personal projection (Asc) that can be accomplished through expansive, unrestricted (♃) visions (♆) and by believing (♃) in the dream (♆)!

- Both Grandma Moses and Wolfgang Amadeus Mozart have ☉ = ☿/♆. They both defined themselves (☉) through use of their imaginative (♆) and artistic communication (☿).

- Though one would anticipate that the Marquis de Sade would have very little in common with Jim Henson, the Marquis is one of the more colorful examples who shares Henson's ☉ = ☿/♆ midpoint picture. The Marquis de Sade's ego-defining (☉) writings (☿) and visions of fantasy (♆) went far beyond what anyone would ever expect to emanate from the lips of Miss Piggy or Kermit the Frog (assuming frogs even have lips).

Although each of these individuals began with the same shared interpretation that we developed for ☉ = ☿/♆, it is fascinating to see how each used the basic interpretation as a starting point and molded it to his or her own purposes.

It quickly becomes obvious that we shouldn't fall into the trap of attempting to over-refine our analysis. If you have a client with ☉ = ☿/♆, then as we saw with the Marquis de Sade's chart, it probably wouldn't be a very good idea to suggest that the client pursue a career of writing about his sadomasochistic fantasies. When using our analytical sentence construction, we must make sense of any interpretation *within the context of the individual client's life* rather than trying to squeeze him into a rigidly defined, restrictive mold of what he should do with his life.

In another example of polarities of interpretation relating to midpoints, consider Adolf Hitler's closest midpoint picture, ♇ = ☉/♃. Using our sentence construction, we would formulate something like this:

The desire to have a major, powerful impact (♇) can be accomplished through an expansive, optimistic (♃) approach to life purpose and ego definition (☉); through illuminated (☉), enthusiastic goals (♃); through unlimited potential; through confidence; and through being aware of the possibility of an inflated (♃) ego (☉).

This interpretation certainly coincides with what we would expect of one of history's most ruthless dictators. But what about other famous people who share this very same midpoint picture? Would we expect them all to be equally depraved in their intentions? Hopefully and mercifully not, although we do see that the mass murderer John Wayne Gacy also has ♇ = ☉/♃, where the Pluto Focal Point takes on a decidedly sexual connotation in addition to the power and force represented by the amalgam of the combined Pluto, Sun, and Jupiter.

It is also interesting to note that British Prime Minister Tony Blair has ♇ = ☉/♃ but that his determination to have a major impact has been used quite differently than in Adolf Hitler's case, further emphasizing the polarities of expression between good and evil through use of the very same influence.

Two famous television evangelists also have this ♇ = ☉/♃ midpoint picture. Oral Roberts uses his high profile to spread the gospel, raise funds, and promote education (Oral Roberts University is aptly named for himself). Jimmy Swaggart enjoyed vast popularity and was a powerful evangelical influence, but struggled with his own personal weaknesses and found that he was not as invincible as this midpoint picture might encourage its owner to believe.

To summarize: Within any measurement—when examined in and of itself—certain responses can reasonably be anticipated. Within these expectations, however, there is always a relatively wide range of potential for individual expression, response, or manifestation. This considerable latitude of expression can be at least partially explained as "free will," the result of conscious decisions, and the conditions of the life environment.

As we go beyond the initial sentence structure that forms the basis for our interpretations, it is fascinating to go deeper to a second level of interpretation. This secondary level of interpretation incorporates the individual's specific talents, interests, and options. As we learn more about a person through conversation during the course of the session, we have the opportunity to make further observations that help us to refine our initial hypothesis. By doing so, we can become aware of potential outlets of activity that fit not only within the range of our astrological expectations, but also within the realistic scope of the client's individual interests and capabilities.

Throughout this book, I have attempted to analyze each midpoint picture from the basic interpretations by utilizing the formula of keywords in the sentence construction technique previously described. After the initial analysis, a second level of interpretation is presented—often detailing and expounding on the preliminary premise. It is my hope that this format will help the reader to become familiar with the method of developing the initial impressions and also to appreciate that the specific means of expression ultimately lies within the individual himself.

---

1. Edison's birth time is unknown, but the Sun, Mercury, and Neptune do not change positions enough throughout a single day to appreciably affect this midpoint picture.

CHAPTER THREE

Significant Midpoints

A hidden connection is stronger than an obvious one.

—HERACLITUS (GREEK PHILOSOPHER, 540–480 BC)

Beginning with the Focal Point

Every Focal Point, even by itself, possesses an inherent symbolic interpretive meaning. This meaning is further refined and modified by the combined symbolic meanings of the planets or points represented in the midpoint on the right side of the equation.

In this section, I'll provide more details about each of the possible Focal Points in the analysis of midpoint pictures. A summary chart of these Focal Points is located in appendix II.

The Sun as the Focal Point

When the Sun is the Focal Point of the midpoint picture, the mechanism for pursuing and potentially accomplishing the life purpose, defining the ego, and solidifying identity is delineated.

- Spiritualist Edgar Cayce's ☉ = ♅/♆ midpoint picture suggests that ego definition (☉) can be accomplished through innovative (♅) or imaginative dreams or visions (♆). This midpoint picture also succinctly defines his identity (☉) in that he was known as the "sleeping (♆) prophet (♅)."

- Carl Jung's ☉ = ☿/♄ midpoint picture suggests that life purpose and ego definition (☉) can be accomplished through putting thoughts and ideas (☿) into a tangible form (♄). Jung's work helped to establish the foundation (♄) for a better understanding of our conscious and unconscious thoughts (☿).

- Sigmund Freud has ☉ = ☿/♇ as one of his midpoint pictures, suggesting a life purpose or ego definition (☉) that can be accomplished through thoughts, ideas, and communication (☿) about profound, deep concepts (♇) and probing (♇) of the mental processes (☿). Freud, who is known widely as the father of modern psychoanalysis, developed numerous theories that involved psychological and sexual issues (♇) and how they were influenced and processed by the mind (☿). Considering that we associate the Focal Point Sun with the ego, it is rather amazing to remember that Freud himself is credited with initially developing the concept of the *ego* in psychotherapy.

- Muhammad Ali's ☉ = ♃/☊ midpoint picture reflects his ego definition (☉) that was possible through his exuberant and effusive (♃) public persona (☊). His trademark statement, "I (☉) am the greatest (♃)," fittingly describes this midpoint picture.

- Ernest Hemingway's ☉ = ♂/♅ sets the tone for his identity and ego definition (☉) that can be accomplished through an energetic, relentless drive (♂) toward individualistic expression (♅). One might also expect an extreme restlessness or volatility (the combination of ♂ and ♅), perhaps associated with heated (♂) outbursts (♅) or reckless (♂) risk taking (♅). Ironically, this same midpoint picture could easily be associated with one of his life's defining works (☉), *A Farewell* (♅) *to Arms* (♂).

- Comedian Woody Allen's ☉ = ♆/Asc midpoint picture suggests that the definition of his ego (☉) can be accomplished through visualization (♆) of personal identity

(Asc). In Allen's case, perhaps an *unclear vision* (♆) of self (Asc) is more appropriate and aptly describes his statement, "My only regret in life is that I wasn't born someone else."

- Noted African explorer David Livingstone's ☉ = ♃/♅ midpoint picture suggests ego definition (☉) that can be accomplished through unrestrained (♃) individualistic (♅) expression or expansive (♃) innovation and exploration (♅).

- Television evangelist Jim Bakker has the midpoint picture ☉ = ♂/♄, which suggests a life purpose or ego definition (☉) that is possible through an energetic and fierce (♂) determination (♄). Appropriate to this midpoint picture is his 1976 autobiography (☉) titled *Move* (♂) *That Mountain!* (♄).

- Mick Jagger, lead singer of the Rolling Stones, has the midpoint picture ☉ = ♀/♄. This midpoint picture suggests that the life purpose, identity, and ego definition (☉) can be accomplished through making aesthetic beauty (♀) tangible (♄). This midpoint picture also aptly describes the Stones' most defining song, which was voted by cable television's VH1 as the number one rock song of all time, "I (☉) Can't Get No (♄) Satisfaction (♀)."

- Heaven's Gate cult leader Marshall Applewhite has the midpoint picture ☉ = ♂/♆, suggesting ego needs (☉) that can be accomplished through charisma or being able to inspire (♆) others to act (♂). Applewhite apparently was charismatic enough to attract others to his fatalistic vision (♆) and inspired (♆) them to their final action (♂) as part of a group suicide.

The Moon as the Focal Point

When the Moon is the Focal Point of the midpoint picture, the mechanism for pursuing and potentially achieving emotional fulfillment is delineated.

- Sigmund Freud's ☽ = ☿/♄ midpoint picture suggests emotional fulfillment (☽) that can be accomplished through giving structure (♄) to thoughts and ideas (☿). We should note that this same midpoint picture could also be interpreted as emotional fulfillment that can be accomplished through an understanding (☿) of repressed (♄) thoughts (☿), an important component of his many pursuits.
- Howard Cosell also has the ☽ = ☿/♄ midpoint picture, which suggests emotional fulfillment (☽) that can be accomplished through giving structure (♄) to thoughts, ideas, and communication (☿). Cosell's compunction for structured, organized thoughts became his motto, "Tell it like it is."
- Walt Disney's ☽ = ♃/♆ midpoint picture points toward emotional fulfillment (☽) possible through expansive, unrestricted (♃) visions (♆)—by believing (♃) in the dream (♆). Another closely related midpoint picture for Disney is ☽ = ♄/♆. This midpoint picture suggests that emotional fulfillment (☽) can be accomplished by giving substance (♄) to the dream (♆)—by making that dream (♆) a reality (♄). Isn't that exactly what cartoon character Jiminy Cricket sang about in "When You Wish Upon a Star"?
- Clint Eastwood's Moon is the Focal Point of his ☽ = ♅/Asc midpoint picture. This suggests that emotional needs (☽) can be accomplished through embracing personal (Asc) individuality (♅) or, alternatively, by personifying the role of an outsider (♅). Many of Eastwood's roles effectively cast him as the loner (♅) or the rebel (♅) with a precariously perched chip on his shoulder. This image is demonstrated in his reckless, independent (♅) personal demeanor (Asc) and is quite evident in his role as Dirty Harry, as well as in the early spaghetti Westerns and other films that have involved his audience emotionally (☽), allowing them to empathize, sympathize, or vicariously identify (Asc) with him.
- Lunar astronaut Neil Armstrong's Moon is involved in two particularly interesting midpoint pictures. The first, ☽ = ♂/♄, suggests that emotional needs (☽) can be accomplished through a fierce (♂) determination (♄) to conquer (♂) obstacles (♄).

The second midpoint picture with the Moon at the Focal Point is ☽ = ♂/♃. This midpoint picture further suggests that emotional needs (☽) can be accomplished through energetic (♂) optimism, expansion, and confidence (♃).

Both these midpoint pictures acquired added significance on July 20, 1969, with Armstrong's famous words that reflected the magnitude of the event as he became the first human to set foot on the lunar (☽) surface: "That's one small (♄) step (♂) for man, one giant (♃) leap (♂) for mankind."

- Film producer David O. Selznick has the midpoint picture ☽ = ♅/♆, which suggests that emotional fulfillment (☽) can be accomplished through innovative (♅), imaginative dreams or visions (♆). Selznick was referred to by some as a "crazy (♅) dreamer (♆)."[1] One of his crowning cinematic achievements was winning the Academy Award for *Gone* (♅) *With the Wind* (♆).

- Entrepreneur Howard Hughes's midpoint picture ☽ = ♅/Mc suggests that his emotional needs can be accomplished through innovative (♅) career (Mc) pursuits. We should note that aeronautics is related to Uranus. This same picture also describes the emotional attitudes (☽) that formed his bizarre, eccentric (♅) public image (Mc).

Mercury as the Focal Point

When Mercury is the Focal Point of the midpoint picture, the mechanism for pursuing and potentially accomplishing efficient thoughts, ideas, and communication is delineated.

- Howard Cosell's ☿ = ♂/Asc midpoint picture suggests that efficient thoughts and communication (☿) can be accomplished through energetic (♂) self (Asc) promotion (♂). Cosell's acerbic (♂) personal style (Asc) of commentary (☿) is reflected in this midpoint picture and also characterizes his self-confidence, or, some might say, overconfidence/arrogance. Another of Cosell's midpoint pictures with Mercury as the Focal Point is ☿ = ♂/♃, suggesting a communication style (☿) that is flamboyant (♃) and reflects opinionated (♃) energy (♂).

- Guyana cult leader Jim Jones has ☿ = ♆/Asc, suggesting that efficient communication (☿) would be either a reflection of self-visualization or an inaccurate or unrealistic (♆) view of (or portrayal of) himself (Asc). Jones's ☿ = ♂/♆ reflects ideas and communication that can be accomplished by using his energy (♂) to promote a new perspective (♆), perhaps even by intimidation. Another of Jones's midpoint pictures that relates to the Focal Point Mercury is ☿ = ♂/♄, which suggests a fierce (♂) determination (♄) or energy (♂) used to gain control (♄).

- Psychic hot line spokeswoman Miss Cleo has the midpoint picture ☿ = ♂/♆, suggesting that efficient thoughts, ideas, and communication (☿) can be accomplished through an energetic (♂) sharing of the vision (♆) or a charismatic demeanor. (Charisma is frequently associated with the ♂/♆ midpoint.) Another interpretation of this midpoint is the use of communication to inspire (♆) to action (♂). While this was certainly the case, as she presented an energetic (♂) and mysterious (♆) image on television commercials, the less savory side of this same midpoint picture also apparently came into play. The ♂/♆ midpoint can also be associated with unclear, veiled, or even deceptive (♆) motives (♂). While her association with the psychic call-in venture proved highly lucrative for a time, it was eventually shut down because of fraudulent (♆) activities (♂).

- Ernest Hemingway's ☿ = ♃/♄ midpoint picture suggests that efficient thoughts, ideas, and communication (☿) can be accomplished through overcoming (♃) limitations (♄), by experiencing extreme ups (♃) and downs (♄)—a theme that is reflected in the title of his novel *To Have* (♃) *and Have Not* (♄) and more broadly in Hemingway's personal life.

- The ☿ = ♄/♅ midpoint picture in Jim Henson's chart suggests that efficient thoughts, ideas, and communication (☿) can be accomplished through breaking (♅) the rules (♄) and gaining stability (♄) through innovative change (♅).

- The magician Roy Horn, of Siegfried and Roy, also has the midpoint picture ☿ = ♄/♅, suggesting that efficient thoughts, ideas, and communication (☿) can be accomplished through breaking (♅) the rules (♄) or bringing structure and organization (♄) to chaos (♅). What could be more appropriate for a person who trains and controls (♄) wild animals (♅)?

Venus as the Focal Point

When Venus is the Focal Point of the midpoint picture, the mechanism for pursuing and potentially accomplishing social, relationship, and aesthetic needs is delineated.

- Singer/songwriter Carole King's midpoint picture ♀ = ♅/ASC suggests that social, relationship, and aesthetic needs (♀) can be accomplished through embracing personal (ASC) individuality and independence (♅). This midpoint picture also brings to light the feelings of social (♀) insecurity (♅) on a personal level (ASC) that may have inspired King's hit song "Will You Still Love Me Tomorrow?"

- Rock Hudson's social, aesthetic, and relationship needs are described by the Venus Focal Point in the midpoint picture ♀ = ☉/♆. While typically suggesting illuminated (☉) imagination or fantasy (♆), for Hudson it may have become less idealistic as it became necessary for him to present an unclear or deceptive image (♆) of who he really was (☉) in order to survive as an actor in Hollywood's social and work environment.

- Oscar-winning producer David O. Selznick's midpoint picture ♀ = ☉/♃ suggests that social, aesthetic, and relationship needs can be accomplished through illuminated (☉), enthusiastic goals, an unlimited (♃) personal potential (☉), and perhaps an inflated (♃) ego (☉) or self-aggrandizement. Selznick had a reputation for his enthusiasm (♃) and arrogance (☉/♃) and was noted for his extravagances (♃).[2]

- Eccentric author Truman Capote's midpoint picture ♀ = ♃/♄ suggests that aesthetic, social, and relationship (♀) needs can be accomplished through overcoming (♃) limitations, obstacles, and restrictions (♄), by pushing (♃) the limits (♄) and stretching (♃) the rules (♄). Among Capote's most famous works was the bestselling 1966 novel *In Cold* (♄) *Blood* (♃).

- When considering midpoint pictures with Venus as the Focal Point, one name that probably wouldn't automatically come to mind is that of Teamster boss Jimmy Hoffa. However, upon closer examination we find that his midpoint picture ♀ = ♂/♇ is rather appropriate. We would expect that social, aesthetic, and relationship (♀) concerns can be accomplished through promotion (♂) of a new perspective (♇), promoting (♂) dramatic change (♇), and perhaps even intimidation (♇). His work (♂) as a labor leader (♇) combines the astrological symbolism of Mars and Pluto represented in the ♂/♀ midpoint to give an image of an intensely (♀) passionate (♂) leader.

- Baseball legend Jackie Robinson's Venus is the Focal Point of the midpoint picture ♀ = ♄/♅, and suggests that social, aesthetic, or relationship needs can be accomplished through breaking (♅) with tradition (♄), by bridging the old (♄) and the new (♅). The social (♀) changes brought about by Robinson's breaking (♅) the color barrier (♄) in professional sports gave society (♀) as a whole a reason to radically part with (♅) outdated (♄) racial attitudes.

Mars as the Focal Point

When Mars is the Focal Point of the midpoint picture, the mechanism for pursuing and potentially accomplishing an efficient use of energy is delineated.

- Walt Disney's midpoint picture ♂ = ♃/♆ suggests that efficient use of energy (♂) can be accomplished through expansive, unrestricted (♃) visions and dreams (♆). This attitude proved instrumental in the creation of the Disney empire.

- Mohandas Gandhi's ♂ = ♀/♇ midpoint picture suggests that an efficient use of energy (♂) can be accomplished through promotion of dramatic social (♀) change (♇). This brings to the forefront the utilization of energy (♂) for a new perspective (♇) and social (♀) transformation (♇). Also of note is Gandhi's midpoint picture ♂ = ♄/Asc, which suggests that an efficient use of energy (♂) can be accomplished through self (Asc) discipline (♄) and self (Asc) restraint (♄), as witnessed by both his legendary fasting and his firm stand (♄) for personal (Asc) values. Yet another example of Mars as the Focal Point of Gandhi's midpoint pictures is ♂ = ♃/♇. This picture suggests that he could efficiently use his energy (♂) in pursuit of his goals (♃), utilizing his strength of conviction and optimism (♃) for sweeping change, empowerment, and transformation (♇).

- Martha Stewart's midpoint picture ♂ = ♃/Mc suggests that an efficient use of energy (♂) can be accomplished through expansive (♃) career (Mc) pursuits and by seeking and expecting public recognition and rewards (♃) for her career (Mc) successes (♃).

- Ernest Hemingway's midpoint picture ♂ = ♄/♆ suggests that efficient use of energy (♂) can be accomplished through giving substance (♄) to the dream (♆). The downside is that it can also strike a cautionary note of possible struggles (♂) with blurred (♆) boundaries (♄) or a clouded (♆) sense of reality (♄). Hemingway received the Pulitzer Prize in 1953 and the Nobel Prize for literature in 1954 for his work (♂) *The Old Man* (♄) *and the Sea* (♆).

- Although we don't know Norman Vincent Peale's exact birth time, his ♂ = ☿/♃ midpoint picture is without doubt still valid. (Please refer to chapter 4 for detailed information regarding the use of midpoints with unknown birth times.) Peale's energy focus (♂) was on expansive, enthusiastic, and optimistic (♃) thoughts, ideas, and communication (☿) and on stretching the boundaries (♃) of the mind (☿). His breakthrough work, *The Power* (♂) *of Positive* (♃) *Thinking* (☿), represents a perfect summation of this midpoint picture.

Jupiter as the Focal Point

When Jupiter is the Focal Point of the midpoint picture, the mechanism for optimism, expansion, and the pursuit of rewards is delineated.

- Charles Chaplin's midpoint picture ♃ = ♄/♆ suggests that expansion (♃) can be accomplished through giving substance (♄) to the dream (♆) or by giving form (♄) to the intangible (♆). Rather remarkably, most of his early rewards and recognition (♃) came from his work in silent (♄) films (♆).

- Sir Winston Churchill's midpoint picture ♃ = ☿/Asc makes the suggestion that rewards and recognition (♃) can be accomplished through introspection (Asc) and communication (☿). Such was his personal communication skill that he was awarded a Nobel Prize (♃) for literature (☿) in 1953.

- Martha Stewart's Jupiter is the Focal Point of the midpoint picture ♃ = ☉/♂. This suggests that optimism, expansion, or possibly excess (♃) can be accomplished through passionate (♂), relentless energy (♂) and self-promotion (☉/♂).

- Frédéric-Auguste Bartholdi, the Italian-French sculptor, has Jupiter as the Focal Point of ♃ = ♀/♅. This midpoint picture suggests that optimism and expansion (♃) can be accomplished through unconventional, unique, or unusual (♅) aesthetic beauty (♀). How appropriate that he received immense recognition (♃) as the designer and builder of the gigantic (♃) Statue (♀) of Liberty (♅) that was located in New York Harbor to greet (♀) immigrants (♅) to the United States.

- The ♃ = ☿/♆ midpoint picture for Elvis Presley suggests that optimism, expansion, and rewards (♃) can be accomplished through communication (☿) used to inspire imaginative dreams or visions (♆), which he accomplished through his music. Ironically, this midpoint picture is also appropriate for one of his biggest (♃) hits, "Suspicious (♆) Minds (☿)."

- The flamboyant performer Liberace's Jupiter in the ♃ = ☉/♅ midpoint picture suggests that expansion, recognition, and rewards (♃) can be accomplished through an innovative, eccentric approach to life purpose (☉) and by bringing attention to, or illumination (☉) of, his individuality or eccentricity (♅).

- Walt Disney's midpoint picture ♃ = ♀/♆ suggests that rewards and recognition (♃) can be accomplished through a beautiful, harmonious (♀) vision (♆). This midpoint picture is evident in his idealistic and enthusiastically pursued vision of Disneyland as being "The Happiest Place on Earth." It is especially ironic that Disney shares this midpoint picture with his earliest creation, Mickey Mouse.[3]

Saturn as the Focal Point

When Saturn is the Focal Point of the midpoint picture, the mechanism for pursuing and potentially establishing necessary controls leading to structure and stability is delineated.

- Guyana cult leader Jim Jones's midpoint picture ♄ = ☽/☿ suggests that structure and stability (♄) can be accomplished through emotional (☽) thoughts, ideas, and communication (☿). Jones was also able to exercise control (♄) over his followers by communicating (☿) emotionally (☽), as this midpoint picture describes. Jones was a skilled communicator, able to persuade others and align them with his thoughts and ideas (☿). His midpoint picture ♄ = ☿/☊ suggests the ability to build structure and stability (♄) through communication and ideas (☿) that are shared with groups (☊). This also describes the ability to control (♄) others through communication (☿) and thus be able to connect with groups (☊) of people and influence their thoughts and ideas (☿).

- Albert Einstein's midpoint picture ♄ = ♃/♆ suggests structure and stability (♄) that can be accomplished through expansive, unrestricted (♃) visions (♆). This midpoint picture also concisely reflects Einstein's comment that "reality (♄) is merely an illusion (♆), albeit a very (♃) persistent (♄) one."

- Agatha Christie's ♄ = ♆/♇ suggests the potential to gain stability and structure (♄) through imagination and visions (♆) and dramatic outcomes (♇). She accomplished this structure (♄) through the creation of her crime (♇) mysteries (♆).

- Sir Winston Churchill's ♄ = ♀/Asc suggests that stability and structure (♄) can be accomplished through being comfortable and at peace (♀) with oneself (Asc), or through personal (Asc) social or aesthetic (♀) pursuits. Churchill possessed artistic talents in addition to his skills as a politician. He frequently painted to calm himself and said, "Were it not for painting (♀), I (Asc) couldn't bear the strain (♄) of things."[4]

- Filmmaker Frank Capra has the midpoint picture ♄ = ♀/Mc, suggesting that structure and stability (♄) can be accomplished through a harmonious or artistic (♀) career (Mc) or through social involvement or exposure (♀) through the career (Mc). Capra was the recipient of multiple Academy Awards, and many of his films share a common thread of tradition, responsibility (♄), and sentimentality (♀). The impact of his films has been so great that a relatively new word has come into common usage. *Capraesque* means "of or evocative of the movies of Frank Capra, often promoting the positive social effects of individual acts of courage."[5]

Uranus as the Focal Point

When Uranus is the Focal Point of the midpoint picture, the mechanism for pursuing and for potentially accomplishing individualistic expression or innovation is delineated.

- José Silva's ♅ = ☿/♃ midpoint picture suggests individualistic expression or innovation (♅) that can be accomplished through expansive, enthusiastic, and optimistic (♃) thoughts (☿), or by stretching (♃) the boundaries of the mind (☿). His innovative (♅) Silva Mind Control program was later renamed Silva Mind (☿) Development (♃). Silva also has the midpoint picture ♅ = ☉/☿. This suggests individualistic expression and innovation (♅) that can be accomplished through illuminated (☉) thoughts and communication (☿).

- Carl Jung's ♅ = ♆/♇ midpoint picture suggests that individualistic or innovative expression (♅) can be accomplished through imagination and visions (♆) to yield dramatic outcomes (♇). This picture also highlights his groundbreaking innovations (♅) for dealing with unconscious (♆) and psychoanalytical (♇) issues. It is also interesting to note that many of his inspirational (♅) breakthrough concepts came from his dreams and visions (♆), which led to a new perspective (♇) in the understanding of psychiatry (♇).

- Miss Cleo, the spokesperson for the call-in psychic network, has ♅ = ☉/♃ as a midpoint picture. This suggests that individualistic expression (♅) can be accomplished through illuminated (☉), enthusiastic goals (♃), but it also carries with it the risk of an inflated (♃) ego (☉) or self-aggrandizement.

Interestingly, the roles with which we identify some actors sometimes show up in the actors' own midpoint pictures. Who knows if this was just pure luck on the part of the casting directors or whether they might have used astrology to choose the actors most likely to personally identify with the roles?

- Robert De Niro's ♅ = ♂/♄ midpoint picture suggests that individualistic expression (♅) can be accomplished through fierce (♂) determination (♄) or frustrated (♄) energy (♂). These traits are shown in his role as the volatile (♅) boxer (♂) Jake La Motta in *Raging* (♂) *Bull* (♄), for which he won the Academy Award for best actor. His role as an ex-Marine loner (♅) driven to violence (♂) in *Taxi* (♅) *Driver* (also ♅) is well-defined by this ♅ = ♂/♄ midpoint picture.

Neptune as the Focal Point

When Neptune is the Focal Point of the midpoint picture, the mechanism for pursuing and potentially accomplishing inspiration, enlightenment, or escape needs is delineated.

- The Dalai Lama XIV has the midpoint picture ♆ = ☉/♃, suggesting inspiration or enlightenment (♆) that can be accomplished through an expansive, optimistic (♃) approach to life and illuminated (☉), enthusiastic goals (♃).

- Saint Teresa of Avila's ♆ = ♃/♅ midpoint picture suggests enlightenment and inspiration (♆) that can be accomplished through expansive (♃) innovation (♅) and exploration (♅). The spirituality associated with Neptune is particularly apt for Saint Teresa's life in that she was associated with numerous (♃) miracles (♅).

  Another of Saint Teresa's midpoint pictures associated with Neptune is ♆ = ☉/♂, which suggests that inspiration (♆) is possible through passionate (☉), relentless energy (♂) in pursuit of life purpose (☉). This midpoint picture also quite eerily illustrates a vision (♆) that she had following an illness in which she stated that a beautiful angel (♆) held "a large golden (☉) dart (♂) and at the end of the iron (♂) tip there appeared to be a little fire (♂). It seemed to me that the angel plunged the dart several times into my heart (☉) and that it reached deep within me. When he drew it out, I thought he was carrying off with him the deepest part of me and he left me all on fire with the great love of God."[6] Though admittedly quite physically painful at the time, the vision left her inspired with a passionate (♂) desire and the direction to fulfill her life purpose (☉).

  As a fascinating follow-up, "Her [Saint Teresa's] heart has been meticulously preserved and kept on display in the Carmelite Church of Alba de Tormes. A surgeon in the late '60s wrote, 'A transverse opening or gash can be noticed in the upper anterior quarter of the heart…it penetrates the tissue and the ventricles…. All along the wound can easily be seen traces of combustion.'"[7]

- Carl Sagan's midpoint picture ♆ = ☿/♇ suggests that inspiration, creative visualization, dreams, or fantasy (♆) can be accomplished through the power (♇) of words (☿) and by communicating (☿) profound (♇), deep concepts and a whole new perspective (♇). Sagan's visionary and inspirational (♆) PBS television series *Cosmos* captivated and educated (☿) millions of viewers as he communicated (☿) his unique perspective (♆) of Earth and beyond.

- Michael J. Fox's ♆ = ♄/♅ midpoint picture suggests inspiration or creativity (♆) that can be accomplished through a break (♅) with tradition (♄). It could equally apply to a fantasy movie (♆) called *Back* (♄) *to the Future* (♅).

- Adolf Hitler's Neptune in the midpoint picture ♆ = ♃/Asc suggests inspiration or creativity (♆) that can be accomplished through self-confidence and showing off (♃) personal (Asc) abilities and talents. Hitler unfortunately gravitated to the much less productive Neptunian expression of confused and delusional visions. Hitler's inflated (♃) ego (Asc) became the vehicle for his self-aggrandizing views.

Pluto as the Focal Point

When Pluto is the Focal Point of the midpoint picture, the mechanism for pursuing and potentially accomplishing or experiencing empowerment, gaining a new perspective, and achieving transformation is delineated.

- M. C. Escher's ♇ = ☽/♆ midpoint picture suggests empowerment, a new perspective, or transformation (♇) that can be accomplished through nurturing of emotional needs (☽) using imagination and fantasy (♆). In hindsight, we could also connect this midpoint picture with a new perspective (♇) through use of optical (☽) illusion (♆).

- Television evangelist Jimmy Swaggart's ♇ = ☉/♃ midpoint picture suggests that empowerment, perspective, and transformation (♇) can be accomplished through illuminated (☉), enthusiastic goals (♃). However, there also exists the possibility of an inflated (♃) ego (☉) or self-aggrandizement with this Sun/Jupiter midpoint.

- Elvis Presley's ♇ = ☿/♀ midpoint picture suggests an empowerment, a new perspective, and transformation (♇) that can be accomplished through beautiful, harmonious, and balanced (♀) communication (☿). Presley truly had a way with words, and his powerful (♇) messages (☿) were harmoniously (♀) delivered.

- Although empowerment, perspective, and transformation (♇) can be accomplished through an illuminated (☉) imagination or dream (♆), as suggested by the ♇ = ☉/♆ midpoint picture, noted transsexual Christine Jorgensen's story also reflects a new perspective and transformation (♇) that is possible through ego or identity (☉) confusion or disorientation (♆).

The North Node as the Focal Point

When the North Node is the Focal Point of the midpoint picture, the mechanism for pursuing and potentially establishing a relationship with the public is delineated. Also, particularly early in life, the North Node as the Focal Point may be indicative of the nature of the relationship with the mother figure.

- Martha Stewart's ☊ = ☉/Asc midpoint picture suggests that the relationship with the public (☊) can be accomplished through confidence, self-centeredness, and an illuminated (☉) identity (Asc).

- Federico Fellini's midpoint picture ☊ = ♅/♆ suggests a connection with the public (☊) that can be accomplished through innovative (♅), imaginative dreams and visions (♆) or through eccentric (♅) fantasy (♆). Fellini's films were unique (♅) and often downright bizarre (♅). It has been said that "he thrived on chaos (♅) and confusion (♆), and his films (♆) are noted for being weird (♅), strange (♆) and exaggerated."[8]

- The father of our country, President George Washington, has the midpoint picture ☊ = ☉/♇, suggesting a relationship with the public (☊) that can be accomplished through powerful (♇) ego (☉) urges, self-assertion, and a need to leave his mark in addition to having a groundbreaking (♇) influence (☉).

- Astronaut John Glenn's midpoint picture ☊ = ♅/Asc suggests a public image (☊) as a free-spirited (♅) individual (Asc). This description fits him well, and in the public view (☊) it describes his identity (Asc) as an adventurer (♅) and as someone willing to take risks (♅).

- Aviator Charles Lindbergh has the midpoint picture ☊ = ♂/♄, which suggests a relationship with the public (☊) that can be accomplished through a fierce (♂) determination (♄) to conquer obstacles. Lindbergh's courageous (♂) solo (♄) flights earned him the nickname "the Lone (♄) Eagle (♂)."

- Christina Crawford, the adopted daughter of Joan Crawford, has two midpoint pictures that demonstrate the maternal connotation of the North Node. Though Christina's birth time is unknown, these midpoint pictures are still applicable. Her ☊ = ☿/♆ midpoint picture suggests a maternal figure (☊) who can exercise influence through inspiring (♆) communication (☿) of imaginative dreams or visions (♆). Christina's autobiographical *Mommie Dearest* suggests a much darker interpretation of this midpoint picture, in which the mother figure (☊) can be influential through confused, distorted, or deceptive (♆) thoughts and communication (☿). Christina Crawford's second midpoint picture with the North Node as the Focal Point is ☊ = ☉/♆, which suggests that the mother figure (☊) can be influential through illuminated (☉) imagination, dreams, or spirituality (♆). Again, based on Christina's accounts, her mother's influence (☊) led to the child's ego and identity (☉) confusion (♆) and a distorted (♆) view of herself (☉).

The Ascendant as the Focal Point

When the Ascendant is the Focal Point of the midpoint picture, the mechanism for pursuing and potentially accomplishing identity definition and a sense of self is delineated. The midpoint picture in this context often speaks volumes about how the individual is viewed by others.

- Martin Luther King Jr.'s midpoint picture Asc = ☉/♆ suggests that his identity definition (Asc) can be accomplished through illuminated (☉) imagination, dreams, or spirituality (♆)—and appropriately describes his memorable, inspiring vision (♆), "I have a dream…"

- Muhammad Ali's Asc = ♅/Mc suggests definition of the ego (Asc) through an eccentric or unpredictable (♅) public image (Mc). His public image (Mc) suffered as he (Asc) was labeled a rebel (♅) and out of the mainstream (♅) for his conscientious objection to military service.

- Sigmund Freud's legacy includes, among other breakthroughs, attempts to interpret dreams. His midpoint picture Asc = ♄/♆ aptly describes how he was able to define himself (Asc) through giving substance (♄) to the dream (♆) and by clarifying (♄) the nebulous (♆).

- With former President Bill Clinton's Asc = ♂/♆, we would expect that identity projection and identity definition (Asc) can be accomplished through an energetic (♂) sharing of a vision (♆) and his personal charisma (♂/♆). This midpoint picture effectively illustrates one of his more memorable quotes in which he expressed his compassion: "I (Asc) feel (♆) your pain (♂)." When we remember that the Mars/Neptune midpoint is notable for a charismatic presentation, we can understand why people are drawn to President Clinton.

- Comedian Steve Martin's midpoint picture Asc = ♃/♅ suggests that identity definition (Asc) can be accomplished through unrestrained (♃) individualistic (♅) expression. In fact, he defined himself (Asc) and gained a reputation with his trademark statement, "I am a wild and crazy guy!" Another appropriate interpretation of the ♃/♅ midpoint is the expression of his unapologetic, opinionated (♃) rebelliousness (♅). That makes perfect sense as we recall his famously indignant and sarcastic, "Well, *excuse* me!"

- President Abraham Lincoln's Asc = ♄/♅ suggests that the identity projection and the definition of identity (Asc) can be accomplished through a clash between the old (♄) and the new (♅) and breaking (♅) with tradition (♄). It is most significant to consider that this midpoint picture could suggest he is identified with the abolition (♅) of slavery (♄). Interestingly, Lincoln's Sun is also identified with this same Saturn/Uranus midpoint, although for the ☉ = ♄/♅ midpoint picture we must extend the orb to 2°02'.

- With his midpoint picture Asc = ♅/♇ suggesting a definition of identity (Asc) that can be accomplished through big changes (♇) for innovation (♅), a radical change (♅) of perspective (♇), and possible disruptive (♅) upheaval (♇), Elvis Presley managed to define himself (Asc) by his new music, which left his young audiences—and their parents—"All Shook Up."

- Andy Warhol's Asc = ☿/♆ midpoint picture suggests a definition of identity (Asc) that can be accomplished through inspiring communication (☿) of imaginative dreams or visions (♆). This midpoint picture is also accurately conveyed in his wittily sarcastic statement, "I'm (Asc) a deeply (♆) superficial (☿) person."

- Jesse Jackson's Asc = ♀/♆ midpoint picture suggests a definition of identity (Asc) that can be accomplished through idealism and harmonious (♀) dreams and visions (♆). Considered by many as a visionary, Jackson's personal affairs demonstrate the concealed activity or deception (♆) in relationships (♀) that is also possible with this midpoint picture. Yet another layer of interpretation for this midpoint picture is his identification with the Rainbow (♆) Coalition (♀) organization.

The Midheaven as the Focal Point

When the Midheaven is the Focal Point of the midpoint picture, the mechanism for pursuing and potentially accomplishing career and professional goals and establishing a public image is delineated.

- President Bill Clinton's midpoint picture Mc = ♂/♆ suggests that his public image can be accomplished through energetically (♂) sharing the dream or vision (♆) or inspiring (♆) action (♂). In this example, the charisma often associated with the Mars/Neptune midpoint shows up in a very public way (Mc).

- Muhammad Ali's Mc = ♂/♄ midpoint picture helps to explain his public (Mc) bravado (♂) and suggests his fierce (♂) determination (♄) to conquer (♂) obstacles (♄).

- Carl Jung's career (Mc) was defined, in large part, by his work with the unconscious (♆) mind (☿). Knowing this, it isn't a surprise to see that he has a midpoint picture of Mc = ☿/♆, suggesting a career or public image (Mc) that can be accomplished through communication (☿) of imaginative dreams or visions (♆).

- Though most widely known for his political career, Sir Winston Churchill's Mc = ☿/♄ suggests another profession. Such was the quality of his career (Mc) of communicating (☿) in a structured and disciplined (♄) way that he received the Nobel Prize for literature in 1953 for his historical (♄) writings (☿) documenting World War II. As an interesting aside, Churchill was publicly (Mc) on record as being linguistically (☿) inflexible (♄), insisting on the most precise (♄) use of language (☿). When asked how he felt about the common—yet technically incorrect—practice of ending a sentence with a proposition, he responded by saying, "It is something up with which I will not put."[9] Still another reference to this same midpoint picture for Churchill is the fact that he struggled (♄) with a speech (☿) impediment (♄).

- Edgar Cayce's career (Mc) consisted of powerful (♇) yet hard-to-define concepts (♆), as shown in his midpoint picture Mc = ♆/♇. This same midpoint picture can be interpreted as a career (Mc) in which imagination and visions (♆) yield dramatic outcomes (♇).

- Judy Garland's Mc = ♃/♆ midpoint picture suggests career (Mc) gains made possible through expansive, unrestricted (♃) visions (♆). While desperately wanting to believe in (♃) the elusive dream (♆), she may have gravitated toward excessive (♃) escapism (♆) rather than what awaited her over (♃) the rainbow (♆).

- Elvis Presley's Mc = ♄/♅ suggests a career that breaks (♅) rules (♄), breaks (♅) with tradition (♄), and allows him to gain stability (♄) through an innovative approach (♅). Another of Presley's midpoint pictures involving the Midheaven as the Focal Point is Mc = ♂/♆, suggesting that his career (Mc) aspirations can be accomplished through his charisma (♂/♆) and energetically (♂) promoting his vision (♆).

The Aries Point as the Focal Point

Special considerations are applicable in situations in which the Aries Point is the Focal Point of a midpoint picture. Please see the section on the Aries Point later in this chapter for a detailed discussion of the specifics of the Aries Point interpretations.

The Sun/Moon Midpoint

Arguably, the Sun and the Moon—the two luminaries—represent the most significant individual components of the natal chart.

In psychological astrology, the Sun represents the individual's ego needs and identity, guiding his life's direction and purpose. The Moon represents the individual's emotional needs—what he needs in his life to feel fulfilled. Together, the Sun and the Moon combine to form what Noel Tyl refers to as the *Sun-Moon Blend*.[10]

The combined influence of and motivation from the Sun-Moon Blend succinctly defines our deepest core values as individuals. These central themes must coexist and seek reinforcing or complementary support from the other planets. These themes are further refined and defined by the Sun's and the Moon's house placement and rulership, and any pertinent midpoint pictures.

Not surprisingly, then, we would expect that the ☉/☽ midpoint would carry with it tremendous importance as it embellishes and solidifies the interaction between the two luminaries. Essentially, the Sun/Moon midpoint represents a microcosm of the needs suggested by the ☉-☽ Blend,[11] bringing together and integrating their collective importance at a specific point in the natal chart.

In fact, the ☉/☽ midpoint will often dominate the life. It adds depth to the interpretation of the ☉-☽ Blend and suggests the level and means of internal continuity between these two all-important influences. Additionally, by defining our most important needs, it also dramatically influences whom we choose to be around—and who chooses to be around us. By doing so, the ☉/☽ midpoint represents an integral factor in determining the participants in all our relationships—whether they are casual, intimate, or professional.

When a Focal Point is within orb of the ☉/☽ midpoint, it undeniably modifies and further defines the core motivations and values represented by the ☉-☽ Blend, and it is important to integrate the resultant midpoint picture(s) into our analysis and synthesis.

The respective signs of the Sun and Moon can add to the interpretation of any midpoint picture that includes the Sun/Moon midpoint. By considering the significant details that the respective zodiac signs of the Sun and Moon contribute, a depth of analysis can be accomplished that is far beyond what would be possible without them. We should remember that the ☉/☽ midpoint represents a microcosm of the needs suggested by the ☉-☽

Blend. **Given the importance of the Sun/Moon midpoint, I routinely consider an orb of 2°30' for this midpoint picture.**

As has already been discussed, potential midpoint pictures in which the Focal Point is also a part of the midpoint on the right side of the equation are deemed meaningless (that is, potential midpoint pictures with the Sun or the Moon as the Focal Point, such as $\odot$ = $\odot/\mathbb{D}$ and $\mathbb{D} = \odot/\mathbb{D}$). **Therefore, the discussion of specific Focal Points in relation to the Sun/Moon midpoint begins with Mercury.**

Mercury at the Sun/Moon Midpoint

When Mercury is the Focal Point of a midpoint picture relating to the ☉/☽, we expect that thoughts, ideas, and communication will be involved as the central unifying focus for the individual, and in his interactions with others.

- With Mercury as the Focal Point of his Sun/Moon midpoint (☿ = ☉/☽), cult leader Jim Jones was able to communicate his thoughts and ideas (☿) in order to gain personal financial and ego security (☉ in ♉). Ironically, this security was attained in large part because Jones was able to persuade many of his followers to renounce all their worldly possessions and donate the proceeds to his cause. Jones was able to attract people to him by forceful communications and by signifying that he was in charge (☽ in ♈).

- Actor and politician Arnold Schwarzenegger also has ☿ = ☉/☽. Communication, thoughts, and ideas (☿) form the central core of his needs. With his Sun in Leo, there is a need to be—figuratively or literally—front and center on the main stage. Schwarzenegger's Moon in Capricorn suggests a determination, a discipline, and an ambitious drive to make things happen in both his acting and his political roles. It may seem more than a bit ironic that a foreign-born movie star with English as a second language has his Mercury—the planet most closely associated with communication—at the Sun/Moon midpoint. However, we must acknowledge that his communication skills are greatly enhanced by the strength of his ego and reputation (☉ in ♌) and his emotional need to administrate and see progress (☽ in ♑). When we consider these facts, it is much easier to understand his success in motion pictures and his unprecedented rise to political power as one of the most powerful public officials at the state level in the entire United States.

- Hugh Hefner has ☿ = ☉/☽, with his Sun in Aries and Moon in Pisces. His assertive drive (☉ in ♈) combines efficiently with a sensitivity and awareness (☽ in ♓) of social trends. Hefner's idea (☿) for the publication of *Playboy* represented a way for him to communicate (☿) his ideals and establish an empire.

Venus at the Sun/Moon Midpoint

When Venus is the Focal Point of a midpoint picture relating to the ☉/☽, we expect that social concerns, aesthetics, or relationships will be involved as a central unifying focus for the individual, and in his interactions with others.

- Former First Lady Eleanor Roosevelt has ♀ = ☉/☽, with her Sun in Libra and Moon in Cancer. Mrs. Roosevelt was immersed in social causes (♀), and her visibility as First Lady allowed her to receive extensive publicity. She assumed an active role while in the White House, balancing (☉ in ♎) her required responsibilities as the wife of the President with social causes that sparked her own emotions (☽ in ♋), particularly women's issues (♀).

- Welsh actor Anthony Hopkins has the midpoint picture ♀ = ☉/☽, with his Sun in Capricorn and Moon in Sagittarius. Hopkins is ambitious and hard working (☉ in ♑), and the artistic expression in his roles is mesmerizing and reflects his strength of conviction (☽ in ♐) for his acting (♀) profession.

- Austrian composer (♀) Franz Joseph Haydn has the ♀ = ☉/☽ midpoint picture. Haydn's Sun in Aries and Moon in Gemini describe his prodigious talent and his tremendously productive career, which elevated him from poverty to the upper echelon of society.

Mars at the Sun/Moon Midpoint

When Mars is the Focal Point of a midpoint picture relating to the ☉/☽, we expect that energy utilization and drive will be the central unifying focus for the individual, and in his interactions with others.

- Boxer Muhammad Ali's Mars at the Focal Point of his Sun/Moon midpoint picture suggests his energetic self-promotion (♂) and highlights the way his ambitious determination (☉ in ♑) combines with his unusual, free-spirited image (☽ in ♒) to help him become one of the world's most beloved athletes.

- Sir Winston Churchill's ♂ = ☉/☽ midpoint describes a potential means of efficient energy utilization (♂) through an ego defined by a powerful strength of conviction (☉ in ♐) and integrated with the emotional need for respect, love, and honor (☽ in ♌). The Sun/Moon midpoint succinctly describes his stellar leadership talents, which helped propel the Allied forces to victory in World War II.

- Real estate entrepreneur Leona Helmsley has Mars at the Sun/Moon midpoint. She developed a reputation as a driven, perhaps ruthless, businesswoman. With her Sun in Cancer, there is little doubt about a need for personal emotional security, but her Moon in Aquarius suggests that she is also a free spirit, quite capable of detaching from her emotions. This combination represented by the ♂ = ☉/☽ midpoint picture reinforces the traits that earned her the nickname "the Queen of Mean."

Jupiter at the Sun/Moon Midpoint

When Jupiter is the Focal Point of a midpoint picture relating to the ☉/☽, optimism, expansion, enthusiasm, and strength of conviction will be the central unifying forces for the individual, and in his interactions with others.

- The Dalai Lama XIV has Jupiter at the Sun/Moon midpoint. Central to his core beliefs and teaching is, "The important thing is that men should have a purpose (♃) in life."[12] His peaceful (♃), smiling countenance shows his compassionate persona (☉ in ♋) combined with an analytical, emotional practicality (☽ in ♍).

- Comedian Steve Martin's ♃ = ☉/☽ aptly describes his trademark manic (♃) performances. His Sun in Leo makes him comfortable in the spotlight, craving and needing the recognition. The intensity suggested by the Moon in Scorpio highlights his sarcastic wit.

- Rock legend Janis Joplin's Jupiter is the Focal Point of her Sun/Moon midpoint picture (♃ = ☉/☽). Her Capricorn Sun suggests the need to work ambitiously and to be in control. However, her Moon in Cancer shows a dramatically different side—one of emotional needs and sensitivity, perhaps an emotional vulnerability—which starkly contrasts with the strong Capricorn drive and ambition. Jupiter dramatically highlights the extremes suggested by these diverse influences—the compulsion for hard work (☉ in ♑) on the one hand and powerful emotional needs (☽ in ♋) on the other—perhaps resulting in emotional (♋) frustration (♑).

- Sports commentator Howard Cosell's ♃ = ☉/☽ midpoint picture clearly defines his enthusiastic, opinionated (♃) viewpoints. The Sun in Aries adds to his assertiveness, while the Moon in Gemini contributes both intellectual abilities and talkative tendencies.

Saturn at the Sun/Moon Midpoint

When Saturn is the Focal Point of a midpoint picture relating to the ☉/☽, control issues or structured restraint will be the central unifying focus for the individual, and in his interactions with others.

- Mohandas Gandhi became an unlikely symbol of structure and stability (♄). Reflecting his need for fairness and harmony (☉ in ♎) as well as for respect and honor (☽ in ♌), Gandhi's Sun/Moon midpoint picture of ♄ = ☉/☽ (orb of 2°05′) helped to define his life of discipline and restraint (♄), and the widespread respect, love, and honor (☽ in ♌) that he earned through peaceful means (☉ in ♎).

- Aviator Charles Lindbergh's Saturn at the ☉/☽ midpoint solidified him as a legend in his own time. With his Sun in Aquarius, he was certainly a free spirit, innovative and adventurous. His Moon in Sagittarius reaffirms his strength of conviction and an unshakable belief in his pursuits. This combination of personal risk taking (☉ in ♒) and strongly held beliefs (☽ in ♐) earned him a place in aviation history. Ironically, this same ♄ = ☉/☽ midpoint picture also accurately reflects the personally damaging and detrimental effects (♄) resulting from Lindbergh's statements that reflected his non-mainstream (☉ in ♒), opinionated beliefs (☽ in ♐) in the buildup to World War II.

- Soviet chess player Garry Kasparov has the midpoint picture ♄ = ☉/☽. He desperately needs to be in control (♄), and his competitive, confrontational (☉ in ♈) attitude and opinionated views (☽ in ♐) combine to make him feel that he is the victim of shenanigans or foul play whenever he loses.

Uranus at the Sun/Moon Midpoint

When Uranus is the Focal Point of a midpoint picture relating to the ⊙/☽, individuality, independence, and freedom will be the central unifying focus for the individual, and in his interactions with others.

- César Chavez's midpoint picture ♅ = ⊙/☽ reflects the expression of innovation and rebelliousness (♅) that was accomplished by his leadership (⊙ in ♈) coupled with his compassion and understanding (☽ in ♓) for the plight of migrant (♅) farm workers.

- Lucille Ball's midpoint picture ♅ = ⊙/☽ demonstrates how she was able to use her individualistic expression (♅) in conjunction with her dramatic Sun in Leo and her ambitious, driven Moon in Capricorn to work hard to achieve what she wanted. Though her television image was zany and unpredictable, Lucy was a serious businesswoman in real life.

- David Koresh, the rebellious leader of the Branch Davidian complex near Waco, Texas, has Uranus at the Sun/Moon midpoint (♅ = ⊙/☽). His Sun in Leo suggests the need to be respected, loved, and honored, and his Moon in Aquarius reinforces his need to be unusual and use unique talents for social change. The Aquarian Moon amplifies the potential impact of Uranus at the focal point of ⊙/☽, suggesting even more eccentricity or nonconformity than either individual influence alone. Koresh proclaimed himself to be the messiah, and made rules for his followers that he himself did not observe. The need to be revered (⊙ in ♌) combined with an uncommon eccentricity (☽ in ♒)—the feeling of not being bound by any rules—help explain some of his motivations.

Neptune at the Sun/Moon Midpoint

When Neptune is the Focal Point of a midpoint picture relating to the ☉/☽, imagination, dreams, or visions will be the central unifying focus for the individual, and in his interactions with others.

- George Lucas's ♆ = ☉/☽ midpoint picture suggests that his imagination, dreams, and visions (♆) can be accomplished through the energies associated with the Sun in Taurus and the Moon in Aquarius. The use of practical energy to build and maintain (☉ in ♉) coupled with the emotional need for innovative, freethinking pursuits (☽ in ♒) create a powerful combination of traits. Lucas's persistence in his early efforts and particularly with the first *Star Wars* movie established him as a force to be reckoned with in the motion picture (♆) industry.

- Another highly respected celebrity in the film industry (♆), Tom Hanks, shares the ♆ = ☉/☽ midpoint picture. He possesses an acting range that would make a chameleon jealous. With the mutual reception of his Cancer Sun and Leo Moon, Hanks's need for emotional security (☉ in ♋) mixes well with his emotional need to be respected, loved, and honored (☽ in ♌). This combination makes him eminently likeable and able to connect with the imagination of the movie (♆) audience on an emotional level.

- Yet another high-profile Hollywood resident also has Neptune at the Sun/Moon midpoint. Nicknamed the "Hollywood Madam," Heidi Fleiss has her Sun in Capricorn and her Moon in Aries. Both ambitious (☉ in ♑) and competitive in her drive to reach the pinnacle (☽ in ♈) in her field, Fleiss pursued her dream (♆) to coordinate clientele for her assemblage of high-priced call girls. The necessarily covert (♆) nature of the operation eventually was exposed, and Fleiss's dream quickly ended.

Pluto at the Sun/Moon Midpoint

When Pluto is the Focal Point of a midpoint picture relating to the ☉/☽, empowerment, perspective, and transformation concepts will be involved as the central unifying focus for the individual, and in his interactions with others.

- Boxer Muhammad Ali's second Focal Point that falls within orb of the Sun/Moon midpoint is ♇ = ☉/☽. This Pluto correlation with the Sun/Moon midpoint carries a tremendous transformative theme. The concept of transformation (♇) permeates both his Sun and his Moon and gives a deeper meaning to the Sun-Moon Blend. By changing both his religion and his name, he symbolically began a new life—akin to the legendary phoenix rising, reborn from the ashes (a dramatic transformation also related to Pluto). By doing so, he gained a new personal focus and stability (☉ in ♑) while exhibiting his willingness to break with the status quo (☽ in ♒) to nourish his individual emotional needs.

- Adolf Hitler also shares the ♇ = ☉/☽ midpoint picture. The transformation (♇) that he envisioned incorporated his ego need to build and maintain his power (☉ in ♉) and his emotional need to control and make things happen (☽ in ♑).

- Dutch artist M. C. Escher has the midpoint picture ♇ = ☉/☽, with both his natal Sun and Moon in the sign of Gemini. The Sun in Gemini is usually associated with communication and diversity, while the Moon in Gemini represents the need for intellectual stimuli. The perspective (♇) encompassed by this Gemini duality is apparent in Escher's work, in which there are often two separate but integrally and perfectly connected visual themes.

The North Node at the Sun/Moon Midpoint

When the North Node is the Focal Point of a midpoint picture relating to the ☉/☽, contacts and interactions with the public will be the central unifying focus for the individual, and in his interactions with others.

- With the North Node at the Sun/Moon midpoint, César Chavez made the most of his assertiveness and leadership skills (☉ in ♈), applying them empathetically (☽ in ♓) as he became a public symbol (☊) in the fight for migrant farm workers' rights.

- The entertainer Cher also has the ☊ = ☉/☽ midpoint picture. She has been able to build and maintain (☉ in ♉) her popularity with the public (☊) in large part due to her hard work and the need to see constant progress (☽ in ♑).

- Director and comedic actor Albert Brooks has the ☊ = ☉/☽ midpoint picture, too. He is at his best when he portrays the well-meaning, sensitive (☉ in ♋), and detail-oriented (☽ in ♍) guy. His characters—such as the burned-out advertising executive who quit his high-paying job to buy an RV and tour the country in *Lost in America*—are likeable sorts, but have nagging insecurities bordering on compulsive neuroses. Perhaps Brooks's popularity stems from the public's ability to see some of its own insecurities and not take them quite so seriously.

The Ascendant at the Sun/Moon Midpoint

When the Ascendant is the Focal Point of a midpoint picture relating to the ☉/☽, identity issues, which include self-projection and self-assuredness, will be the central unifying focus for the individual, and in his interactions with others.

- Arnold Schwarzenegger has his Ascendant at the Sun/Moon midpoint. His identity definition (ASC) can be accomplished through his Sun in Leo (the hero role) coupled with his Moon in Capricorn (emotional, ambitious determination). The two combined influences create a high level of personal confidence (☉ in ♌) and the discipline and determination (☽ in ♑) necessary to make him a formidable force.

- General George Patton's self-assurance, suggested by his midpoint picture of ASC = ☉/☽, was quite evident in his life. With his Sun in Scorpio suggesting ego (☉) intensity (♏) and his Moon in Capricorn suggesting an emotional (☽) discipline and determination (♑), the result was a no-holds-barred, win-at-any-cost personal attitude.

- Howard Cosell, with his Aries Sun and Gemini Moon, has ASC = ☉/☽. This midpoint picture dramatically emphasizes Cosell's assertive, aggressive (☉ in ♈), and verbose (☽ in ♊) style, which came through loud and clear in his self-assured projection of himself (ASC) and his views.

The Midheaven at the Sun/Moon Midpoint

When the Midheaven is the Focal Point of a midpoint picture relating to the ☉/☽, the expectation is that the public image and career will be the central unifying focus for the individual, and in his interactions with others.

- Actor James Dean's Mc = ☉/☽ characterizes his public image (Mc) as a restless, free-spirited individual (☉ in ♒) with a pronounced brooding emotional intensity (☽ in ♏) that helped define his cinematic mystique and appeal.

- Comedienne Lucille Ball has the midpoint picture Mc = ☉/☽, suggesting the ego need to be recognized (☉ in ♌), which is perfect for a performer. Her Moon in Capricorn suggests the drive, ambition, and hard work that propelled her professional success.

- Famed British poet (♀) Elizabeth Barrett Browning has Mc = ♀ = ☉/☽. Her creative (♀) career (Mc) stemmed from her extreme sensitivity (☉ in ♓), which was expressed so beautifully (☽ in ♎) in her poetry, particularly in her love sonnets (♀).

The Ascendant/Midheaven Midpoint

Perhaps second only to the Sun/Moon midpoint in overall importance is the Ascendant/ Midheaven midpoint. This point connects the two most important *angles* of the natal chart and brings the two together. For a better understanding of this significant midpoint, a preliminary discussion is useful.

The Ascendant

Intimately associated with our definition and expression of personal identity as well as our outer expression of self, the Ascendant is all about how we present ourselves—or perhaps more accurately how others perceive us. These multifaceted perceptions that others make about us are often related to their first impressions and can have a significant effect on how effectively and successfully we will be able to interact with others.

Until people get to know us well, initial impressions speak volumes about us. Our speech and use of grammar, physical appearance, posture, mannerisms, style and choice of clothing, grooming, and so forth all combine to project a level of confidence (or lack thereof) or an air of authority (or passivity) that people use as they assess, develop, and process their initial opinions of who we appear to be. Consciously or unconsciously, initial observations tell others whether they would like to be around us—or not.

While the old proverb "You can't judge a book by its cover" is widely believed and generally accepted as the truth, many of us act counter to that sage advice. It is just human nature to evaluate everyone we meet in varying degrees of detail. Perhaps this behavior goes back as far as early man, where a rapid assessment of whether an individual was perceived as a friend or as a potential threat could quickly become a matter of life and death. While most people we meet today normally do not pose an imminent threat, it is still to our advantage to be able to formulate and assimilate as much information as possible about them as quickly as possible.

The Midheaven

The Midheaven is intimately associated with our most public image and is very often closely associated with our chosen profession or career. The Midheaven symbolizes our spoken or unspoken response to the question "What do you do for a living?" Our Midheaven helps people categorize us, to file us with others stored in their mental data bank. Correct or not, these impressions form the basis of how we are publicly perceived.

Our past associations and experiences—with lawyers, plumbers, used-car salesmen, bankers, doctors, artists, insurance salesmen, and almost every other conceivable professional—help us to determine how much respect, ambivalence, or contempt we assign to a person's career.

While few of us would openly admit it in this age of political correctness, we quickly make judgments based on both the physical appearance and the career of any new acquaintance. Prejudgment (the origin of the word *prejudice*) allows us to rapidly associate and assign our own personal hierarchical value judgments regarding what the person is like until we have a chance to know him better.

Before we proceed, please let me offer another, slightly different perspective on the Ascendant and Midheaven contrast/relationship. I try to think of the Ascendant as what others observe about us when we are not necessarily aware that they are watching. Following this same line of reasoning, the Midheaven is what we choose to show others about ourselves when we are fully aware that we are being observed, the spotlights are on, and the cameras are rolling.

Significance of the Ascendant/Midheaven Midpoint

Regardless of the specific definitions we choose for the Ascendant and Midheaven, the Ascendant/Midheaven midpoint links together our personal identity with our public image to form a symbiotic—and ideally a synergistic—relationship. The more compatible or congruous these two points are, the greater our potential for being "at one" with ourselves.

While some people might genuinely thrive on the dramatic contrast of a Jekyll and Hyde relationship between the Ascendant and the Midheaven, it's probably safe to say that most of us would find it preferable to have some substantial common ground between the two. Regardless of their inherent differences, the Ascendant/Midheaven midpoint represents an area of the chart where our personal and public sides can come together and figuratively reach a happy medium. This may involve some give and take between these two powerful angles and require some balance or compromise to acknowledge and appease both.

If a Focal Point is within orb of the Ascendant/Midheaven midpoint, it suggests and identifies a significant way for the two angles to peacefully and productively coexist, whether they form a mutually beneficial alliance or instead play creatively on their collective diversity.

The Focal Point of the Asc/Mc midpoint picture may act as a virtual bridge between the Ascendant and Midheaven, allowing an interplay of different motivations.

The following examples relate to specific Focal Point involvement in pictures with the Ascendant/Midheaven as the midpoint. **As with the Sun/Moon midpoint, when I evaluate Ascendant/Midheaven midpoints I routinely extend the orb to 2°30'.** In this section, names followed by an asterisk indicate that the orb connecting the Focal Point and the Asc/Mc midpoint is greater than 2° but not greater than 2°30'.

☉ = *Asc/Mc*

When the Sun is located at the Asc/Mc midpoint, the pursuit of ego definition and life purpose seeks a consistency through both the personal identity and the public image. While a certain degree of contentment may come with the unity of focus suggested by this placement, at times it may seem that the life is being lived under a virtual magnifying glass, with the intensity of the Sun's focus a source of incessant scrutiny and heat.

Famous people with this placement include actress Joan Crawford, former President John F. Kennedy, writer F. Scott Fitzgerald, *Hogan's Heroes* actor Bob Crane,* and *Superman* star Christopher Reeve.*

☽ = *Asc/Mc*

When the Moon is located at the Asc/Mc midpoint, individuals typically are able to easily elicit or provoke an emotional response in the people around them. While emotional feelings may be particularly easy to express, it may also be quite difficult to conceal heartfelt emotions.

Famous people with this placement include pilot Amelia Earhart, actor James Dean, comedian John Belushi, country music singer Johnny Cash, magician David Copperfield, singer-songwriter Carole King, Hollywood Madam Heidi Fleiss, former President Bill Clinton, Senator Jesse Helms Jr., Michel de Nostradamus, accused murderer Lizzie Borden,* and musician Bob Dylan.*

☿ = *Asc/Mc*

When Mercury is located at the Asc/Mc midpoint, thoughts, ideas, and communication come naturally. It is easy to talk with people—and to have them listen attentively. The power of communication is emphasized and is often highly developed and refined. Somehow people are as drawn to the communication style in the delivery of the message as with the songs of Homer's Sirens. There may also be deep analytical introspection in an attempt to figure out where (or if) one belongs.

Famous people with this placement include actors Dustin Hoffman, River Phoenix, and Marlon Brando, convicted murderer Jeffrey Dahmer, television evangelist Tammy Faye Bakker, musician David Bowie, the entertainer Cher, sportscaster Howard Cosell, noted transsexual Christine Jorgensen, and psychologist Carl Jung.*

♀ = Asc/Mc

When Venus is located at the Asc/Mc midpoint, aesthetic, social, and relationship needs are integral to identity contentment. There is often an inherent attractiveness (although not always on a physical level) and a likeability that permeates the identity.

Famous people with this placement include actors Mickey Rooney and Sissy Spacek, singer-songwriter Karen Carpenter, and actor-director Clint Eastwood.

♂ = Asc/Mc

When Mars is located at the Asc/Mc midpoint, the identity often needs to be associated with taking action, for bravery, for courage, for self-promotion, or for leadership qualities. There may be a tendency toward impulsive or assertive behavior.

Famous people with this placement include puppeteer Jim Henson, Heaven's Gate cult leader Marshall Applewhite, actor Harrison Ford, pilot Amelia Earhart, tobacco industry critic Jeffrey Wigand, would-be presidential assassin John Hinckley, *Playboy* publisher Hugh Hefner,* the entertainer Cher,* actor James Dean,* and alternative musician Kurt Cobain.*

♃ = Asc/Mc

When Jupiter is located at the Asc/Mc midpoint, the identity is expansive, optimistic, outgoing, enthusiastic, generous, and perhaps committed to a cause. There may be a larger-than-life projection of the identity, such as exaggerated, over-the-top behavior, in an attempt to call attention to oneself.

Famous people with this placement include author and physician Deepak Chopra, Jesse Jackson, television evangelist Jimmy Swaggart, singer and actress Tina Turner, metaphysician

Edgar Cayce, Italian singer Andrea Bocelli, pilot Amelia Earhart, psychiatrist Sigmund Freud, and producer-director Steven Spielberg.*

♄ = Asc/Mc

When Saturn is located at the Asc/Mc midpoint, there is an identification with control issues. Individuals may insist on being in charge and proceed ambitiously, or may instead be extremely cautious, patient, and reserved.

Famous people with this placement include Indian statesman Mohandas Gandhi, television evangelist Jim Bakker, actress Mae West, musicians David Crosby and Bob Dylan, chess master Bobby Fischer, actor Rock Hudson, psychiatrist Sigmund Freud, and producer-director George Lucas.*

♅ = Asc/Mc

When Uranus is located at the Asc/Mc midpoint, individuality, innovation, eccentricity, or even rebelliousness can be intimately associated with the individual's identity. This placement can sometimes make its owner feel out of the mainstream or otherwise alienated because he doesn't fit into the normal, traditional mold. In extreme cases, there can be reckless or excessive risk-taking behavior, perhaps even of a self-destructive nature.

Famous people with this placement include Sir Winston Churchill, artist Pablo Picasso, actress Sharon Tate, tobacco industry critic Jeffrey Wigand, musician Jerry Garcia, Branch Davidian leader David Koresh, Hollywood gossip columnist Rona Barrett, heiress Patty Hearst,* astrologer Noel Tyl,* and baseball's Pete Rose.*

♆ = Asc/Mc

When Neptune is located at the Asc/Mc midpoint, the identity often relates to idealistic, spiritual, or inspirational values. Alternatively, there may be an unclear self-image or, in extreme cases, perhaps even an attempt to conceal the true identity or deceive the public. There may also be nebulous identity issues swirling beneath the surface, suggesting that there may be something more than meets the eye.

Famous people with this placement include actresses Joan Crawford and Judy Garland, boxer Muhammad Ali, football player and actor O. J. Simpson, cult leaders Jim Jones and Charles Manson, the Marquis de Sade, talk show host Oprah Winfrey, comedians Bill Cosby and Jonathan Winters, and musician David Bowie.*

♇ = *Asc/Mc*

When Pluto is located at the Asc/Mc midpoint, the identity may be involved in power struggles, perhaps in an attempt to make a dramatic impact or to transcend problems. There may be an intense focus on self-empowerment, on gaining a new perspective, or on personal transformation.

Famous people with this placement include humorist Will Rogers Sr., artist Edouard Manet, King Ludwig II of Germany (Mad Ludwig), Chris Farley of *Saturday Night Live*, poet Emily Dickinson, beating victim Rodney King, and actors River Phoenix, Bob Crane, and Ruth Gordon.

It is difficult to read this celebrity list without being reminded of Pluto's association with death. Those in this list that met with premature death include Farley, Phoenix, and Crane. Very suspicious circumstances also surrounded the death of King Ludwig II. Even though Ruth Gordon died of natural causes, one of her most memorable films, *Harold and Maude*, was focused on the topic of death.

☊ = *Asc/Mc*

When the North Node is located at the Asc/Mc midpoint, public exposure comes easily and may be almost unavoidable. Others may perceive that the welcome mat is always out. One may even feel as though one is perpetually on display, much like a person living in a glass house. One must remain acutely and vigilantly aware that any potential missteps or indiscretions will likely be brought to the public's attention.

Famous people with this placement include Walt Disney, evangelist Jim Bakker, Jesse Jackson, Oprah Winfrey, comedian Woody Allen, musician Jerry Garcia, actors Dustin Hoffman and Kathy Bates, psychologist Carl Jung, beating victim Rodney King, opera legend Enrico Caruso, the Psychic Friends Network's "Miss Cleo," LSD guru Timothy Leary,* director Frank Capra,* and the severely immune-deficient "Bubble Boy" David.*

AP = *Asc/Mc*

When the Aries Point is at the Asc/Mc midpoint, the potential for public projection is amplified by the public through identity display. Please see the section on the Aries Point later in this chapter for a detailed discussion of this midpoint picture.

One Final Asc/Mc Scenario

In cases where Asc/Mc = ☉/☽, there is a unity of focus with substantial common ground connecting the ego, emotional needs, and the expression of identity—both on a personal level and through the public image or the career.

Under normal circumstances during the course of natal midpoint analysis, if a midpoint doesn't fall within orb of any focal point, we justifiably dismiss it from consideration. However, there is one situation in which I feel compelled to make an exception. This occurs in comparatively rare cases wherein both of the "big two" midpoints—the Sun/Moon and the Ascendant/Midheaven—are within orb of one another.

Famous people with this placement include actor Sean Connery, Walt Disney, producer David O. Selznick, astrologer Noel Tyl, author Ernest Hemingway, and British Prime Minister Tony Blair.

Midpoint Pictures and Unaspected Planets

Defining "Unaspected"

Aspects—the specific angular relationships between planets—help us to better understand how the planets' specific energies will potentially interrelate and interact with one another.

But frequently we encounter charts in which an individual planet is not connected to any other planet by a major aspect.[13] How should we approach these situations? The initial impulse might be to just dismiss them and move on. But if we do so, then we are missing out on a tremendously important dynamic of the horoscope.

While orbs are largely a matter of personal choice, the parameters that I use are shown in figure 7. You will notice that I use rather tight orbs and in most cases allow a slightly larger orb when either the Sun or the Moon is involved in a specific aspect.

Ptolemaic Aspect	Glyph	Degrees of Separation	Orb (with ☉ or ☽)	Orb (without ☉ or ☽)
Conjunction	☌	0°	7°	5°
Sextile	✶	60°	3°	3°
Square	□	90°	7°	5°
Trine	△	120°	7°	5°
Opposition	☍	180°	7°	5°

Figure 7. Suggested Ptolemaic Orbs

Merely because an unaspected planet isn't well integrated within the rest of the chart hardly suggests that the planet must remain quietly on the sidelines as a passive observer. Rather than being content with this segregated astrological isolation, the unaspected planet is often compelled to act up or make some noise in order to gain notice and promote its own agenda as suggested by its particular sign and house placement. We routinely see that these unaspected "renegades"—which aren't intimately wired into the circuitry with the rest of the planets—may have to struggle or fight to become involved or to receive their due recognition.

Several interpretive techniques can help us understand unaspected planets. These methods include the utilization of minor aspects, house rulerships,[14] mutual receptions,[15] and *midpoint pictures.* Although all these techniques are less obvious links than those normally associated with a major aspect, these connections help us to become aware of alternative mechanisms by which the unaspected planet can become more intricately and intimately involved in the overall chart dynamics. What we are looking for is a way to identify and understand these potential interactions between planets that don't have any inherent, obvious connections by major natal aspect.

Using Midpoint Pictures with Unaspected Planets

When utilizing midpoints in the analysis of unaspected planets, the initial approach is to consider all midpoint pictures that involve the unaspected planet as the Focal Point (within a 2° orb) in the midpoint picture equation.

Typically, the analysis of an unaspected Focal Point begins with virtually the same basic interpretation that was discussed in chapter 2. The difference is that due to the astrological isolation, the unaspected planet may have a confrontational celestial chip on its shoulder. If there were a cosmic report card, then in the section titled "Plays well with others," the grade would likely be "some improvement needed." Neither is the unaspected planet likely to be content in a background position or in a subservient role, particularly if the unaspected Focal Point is one of the aptly named *personal planets*.[16]

As an example, consider that an unaspected Sun in Leo located in the tenth house and ruling the tenth could easily describe a situation in which the abundant ego energy is desperately searching for a suitable public forum to "strut his stuff" and gain public exposure.

Then, if we see that the Sun forms a natal quintile[17] with the Ascendant, we get the feeling that projecting this strong public persona (☉ in ♌) is essential to creating and defining a sense of self (Asc).

Continuing with our example, creativity is further emphasized by a midpoint picture involving the unaspected Sun, in which Sun = Mercury/Neptune suggests that identity definition and ego needs (☉) can be accomplished through thinking and communicating (☿) imaginatively (♆) or perhaps by formulating (☿) a strategy (♆).

The example in the preceding paragraphs is from the chart of Napoleon Bonaparte I and demonstrates that while an unaspected planet may not inherently have a *direct* means to connect with the rest of the chart, it is often of paramount importance that it find a way to be noticed. In this manner, the unaspected planet frequently becomes involved as an important part of a central developmental theme.

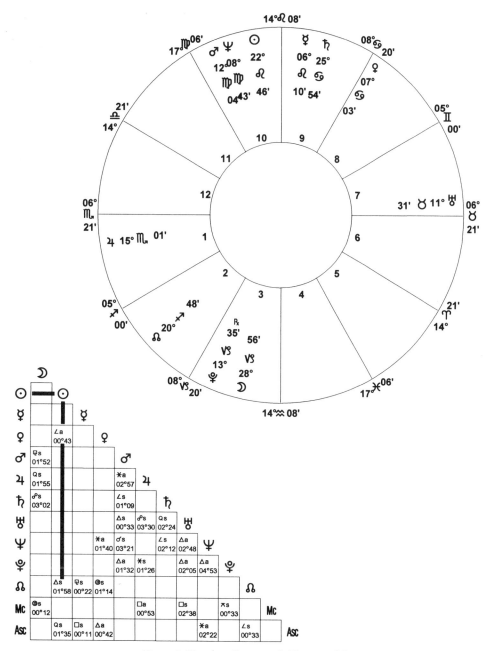

Figure 8. Napoleon Bonaparte's Unaspected Sun

Napoleon Bonaparte
August 15, 1769 / Ajaccio, Corsica / 11:30 AM LMT
Placidus Houses

As we can see from the aspect grid in Napoleon's chart in figure 8, the only aspect from the Sun *to another planet* is the semisquare to Venus. The semisquare is a minor aspect, and for our purposes we consider a planet unaspected only if it makes *no major (Ptolemaic) aspect* to another planet. Also, the trine to the North Node doesn't matter for the unaspected planet analysis because the aspect must be to *another planet*.

In the relatively uncommon situations in which we find that the unaspected planet is not the Focal Point within orb of any midpoint pictures, we can reasonably extend the orb from 2°00' to 2°30' to gain insight into the unaspected planet.

The following section delineates specific unaspected planets as Focal Points in midpoint pictures. Each unaspected Focal Point is described and then illustrated by examples using famous people. A concise table for interpretation of unaspected planets as Focal Points is included in appendix IV.

Unaspected Sun

When the Sun is unaspected, the individual must work particularly hard to define the ego and determine the direction of his life pursuits. The challenge is in deciding where to focus one's energy.

- Hollywood gossip columnist Rona Barrett's midpoint picture of ☉ = ♀/♆ gives some additional meaning to her unaspected Sun by suggesting that ego needs and definition of identity can be accomplished through a harmonious (♀) vision (♆) or social (♀) affairs and activities behind the scenes (♆).

- Charles Chaplin's unaspected Sun is represented in the midpoint picture ☉ = ☽/☿, demonstrating that ego definition can be accomplished through emotional thoughts and communication. Remember that Chaplin's early work was in silent films. Still, he was able to identify (☉) with the audience on an emotional level (☽) through a medium in which traditional communication (☿) was impossible at that time.

- Mohandas Gandhi has the midpoint picture ☉ = ♄/☊ representing his unaspected Sun as the Focal Point. This picture suggests that his life purpose and definition of ego (☉) can be accomplished through having a tangible, stabilizing, or controlling effect (♄) on the public (☊). This same midpoint picture is also quite appropriate for his image of showing public (☊) restraint (♄).

Unaspected Moon

When the Moon is unaspected, the individual must work particularly hard to understand and pursue his emotional needs. The challenge is to find a way to integrate these emotional needs effectively with other personality traits.

- Rock Hudson's unaspected Moon is the Focal Point of his $\mathcal{D} = ♀/♂$ midpoint picture. This picture highlights his emotional needs ($\mathcal{D}$) that can be accomplished through use of energy ($♂$) for an aesthetic ($♀$) purpose, and an emphasized sexual energy. Hudson's likeable motion-picture persona appealed to both males and females in his roles as a hero and as a romantic lead. The same midpoint picture that allowed him to identify with both sexes professionally may also have been related to personal emotional ($\mathcal{D}$) and sexual ($♀/♂$) issues that he felt compelled to conceal.

- Louis Pasteur's unaspected Moon is the Focal Point of his $\mathcal{D} = ♃/♅$ midpoint picture, which suggests the emotional need ($\mathcal{D}$) to use expansive, innovative ($♃$) exploration and innovation ($♅$). Pasteur's enthusiastic ($♃$) passion for research led to groundbreaking ($♅$) work with diseases and preventive medicine.

- Tom Hanks's unaspected Moon is the Focal Point of his $\mathcal{D} = ☿/♂$ midpoint picture, suggesting that emotional needs ($\mathcal{D}$) can be accomplished through energetic, assertive, or forceful ($♂$) thoughts, ideas, and communication ($☿$). Hanks's acting skills are able to stir the emotions in his audiences. With characters ranging from Forrest Gump to the lawyer dying of AIDS in *Philadelphia*, Hanks finds a way to emotionally and forcefully deliver his characters' messages.

Unaspected Mercury

When Mercury is unaspected, the individual must work particularly hard to integrate his thoughts, ideas, and communication with his talents and his potential. The challenge is to be analytical and thorough without becoming obsessed with perfection, and to embrace diversity without becoming scattered and spreading oneself too thin.

- Mohandas Gandhi's unaspected Mercury is the Focal Point of the midpoint picture ☿ = ♂/♆. In addition to the charisma typically associated with the Mars/Neptune midpoint, this picture could also describe how efficient thoughts, ideas, and communication (☿) are possible through an energetic (♂) sharing of the dream or vision (♆) and being inspired (♆) to take action (♂).

- Actor Tom Hanks's unaspected Mercury shares the same ☿ = ♂/♆ midpoint picture with Gandhi. Hanks possesses a large dose of charisma that is apparent in his communication both on and off the big screen.

- Actor Rock Hudson's Mercury is unaspected and figures in the ☿ = ♀/♄ midpoint picture. This picture suggests that efficient thoughts and communication (☿) can be accomplished through making aesthetic beauty (♀) tangible (♄), as demonstrated by his lavish estate. Unfortunately, it also alludes to a possible need to exercise social (♀) caution or reserve (♄) when communicating (☿).

Unaspected Venus

When Venus is unaspected, the individual must work particularly hard to understand and integrate aesthetic and social needs into his life. The challenge is to find harmony and contentment in one's surroundings and relationships.

- Judy Garland's unaspected Venus has no midpoint pictures within a 2° orb, but if we extend the range to 2°30', then Venus is the Focal Point of the midpoint picture ♀ = ☽/♆ (within an orb of 2°27') and suggests that her social, aesthetic, and relationship needs (♀) may be influenced by an idealistic and profoundly emotional (☽) sensitivity (♆), perhaps resulting in emotional (☽) confusion or disorientation (♆). The social sensitivity (vulnerability?) is further emphasized by her unaspected Venus's placement in Cancer.

- Entrepreneur extraordinaire Martha Stewart's unaspected Venus arguably has inspired and driven her to the status of preeminent expert in civilized home decorating and entertaining. The midpoint picture ♀ = ♂/♇ highlights her intense (♇) passion (♂) for all things social (♀). Stewart has effectively used her energy (♂) to bring about a new perspective and transformation (♇) of social (♀) pursuits for innumerable devotees. Innovative (♅) expansion (♃) of her empire has included publishing (♃) her own magazine and relates to the unaspected Venus by way of the ♀ = ♃/♅ midpoint picture.

- Arnold Schwarzenegger's unaspected Venus plays a role in the midpoint picture ♀ = ☊/Mc. Social, aesthetic, and relationship needs (♀) can be accomplished through working with the public (☊) in a career (Mc) utilizing a high-visibility, high-profile public image. In his acting career and later in his political career, he has savored publicity and has flourished in the public spotlight.

- Mae West's unaspected Venus is the Focal Point of the ♀ = ♄/♅ midpoint picture. Her stage and film presence broke (♅) with tradition (♄) as she helped to relax some of society's (♀) values regarding sexuality and social interactions.

- Pablo Picasso's midpoint picture ♀ = ♅/Mc prominently features an unaspected Venus. This suggests social and aesthetic (♀) expression through an unconventional or innovative (♅) career (Mc). Picasso was nothing if not innovative in his art. It appears that his aesthetic focus changed frequently and radically (♅) based on what he was experiencing and feeling at the time. These shifts allowed his creations to maintain a freshness with each successive phase, and in the process kept both the artist and the art aficionados interested and stimulated.

Unaspected Mars

When Mars is unaspected, the individual must work particularly hard to find a productive and fulfilling outlet for his energy. The challenge is to find a constructive way to use this energy rather than gravitating toward impulsiveness or anger.

- Rock Hudson's unaspected Mars figures prominently in the ♂ = ♀/♆ midpoint picture. The efficient use of energy (♂) that was developed and utilized to create an image of idealism and a beautiful (♀) dream (♆) eventually required that considerable energy (♂) be expended to maintain a social (♀) camouflage (♆) to conceal (♆) aspects of his personal life.

- Janis Joplin's unaspected Mars is the Focal Point of the midpoint picture ♂ = ♃/♅, suggesting that her energy (♂) is directed toward unrestrained (♃) individualistic (♅) expression. This midpoint picture suggests the reckless (♃), devil-may-care, risk-taking (♅) attitude that defined her too-brief life.

- Oscar-winning film producer David O. Selznick's unaspected Mars is the Focal Point of the midpoint picture ♂ = ♀/♇, suggesting energy utilization that can be accomplished through aesthetic or social (♀) transformation (♇) or a new aesthetic (♀) perspective (♇).

Unaspected Jupiter

When Jupiter is unaspected, the individual must work particularly hard to find a productive outlet for his enthusiasm while avoiding the risk of excess. The challenge is to use optimism and strength of conviction in an expansive yet realistic pursuit.

- Actress Joan Crawford's unaspected Jupiter is the Focal Point in the midpoint picture ♃ = ☽/♂, suggesting the pursuit of expansive or excessive rewards (♃) through emotional (☽) actions (♂), or possibly emotional (☽) outbursts or tantrums (♂).

- In addition to Janis Joplin's unaspected Mars, she also has unaspected Jupiter in the midpoint picture ♃ = ♀/♂, suggesting rewards or possible excesses (♃) that are possible through the energetically (♂) aesthetic (♀) delivery of her music through her unrestrained (♃), raw (♂) vocals (♀). Her lyrics encourage enthusiastic (♃) pursuit of social (♀) urges (♂) while reinforcing and giving a sexual charge (♀/♂) to her message to "Get It While You Can."

- In a classic example of unaspected Jupiter, we find the midpoint picture ♃ = ♅/Asc, suggesting that rewards, recognition, or excess (♃) can be accomplished through embracing personal (Asc) individuality and eccentricity (♅). The owner of this picture is the famed Hollywood swashbuckler Errol Flynn. Flynn received recognition and financial rewards for his flair for adventure (♅) that helped to define his personal image (Asc). A notorious free spirit (♅), Flynn had an unrestrained (♃) lifestyle that was well documented and included frequent rule-breaking (♅) personal (Asc) behavior. Flynn said, "My problem lies in reconciling my gross habits with my net income."[18]

- President Abraham Lincoln's unaspected Jupiter forms the midpoint picture ♃ = ☿/♀, which suggests optimism and expansion (♃) that can be accomplished through harmonious, balanced (♀) communication (☿) and through having a way with words. Lincoln was a skilled orator, and his ability to assemble and deliver words to achieve the maximum impact is legendary.

Unaspected Saturn

When Saturn is unaspected, the individual must work particularly hard to establish or adapt to necessary controls. The challenge is to maintain a balance between stability, structure, determination, and discipline on the one hand and inflexibility, stubbornness, and austerity on the other. All work and no play...

- Jimmy Swaggart has Saturn as the Focal Point in the midpoint picture ♄ = ☿/♆, suggesting that structure and stability can be accomplished through communication (☿) used to inspire, perhaps spiritually (♆). Unfortunately, the downside of this midpoint picture suggests controlling (♄) others through distorted or deceptive (♆) communications (☿).

- The unaspected Saturn in Geraldo Rivera's chart has no midpoints within a 2° orb, but creates the midpoint picture ♄ = ♅/Mc when the orb is extended to 2°08'. This midpoint picture suggests that structure and stability (♄) can be accomplished through an innovative (♅) public image (Mc) or public risk taking. It is interesting to note that Uranus is also associated with television.

- Pete Rose's quest for a lasting place in the public view is complicated by his unaspected Saturn. The midpoint picture ♄ = ♆/Mc (using an orb of 2°02') suggests an unclear (♆) public image (Mc) and perhaps even stubbornness or austerity (♄). This perception may reinforce an impression of public (Mc) deception (♆) that could diminish Rose's chance to eventually be voted into the Baseball Hall of Fame.

Unaspected Uranus

When Uranus is unaspected, the individual may have to work particularly hard to feel comfortable with the expression of his individuality. The challenge is to be able to find a constructive outlet for unconventional energies and to express—rather than suppress—individuality while avoiding any unnecessarily disruptive or even self-destructive paths.

- John F. Nash's *(A Beautiful Mind)* unaspected Uranus forms a midpoint picture of ♅ = ☉/Asc (orb of 2°23'), which suggests that individualistic expression (♅) can be accomplished through self-discovery (☉/Asc) and a clarification (☉) of identity (Asc).

- John Belushi's unaspected Uranus is involved in the midpoint picture ♅ = ☿/☊ and is just slightly beyond our normal orb at 2°03'. This picture suggests that individualistic expression or innovation (♅) can be communicated (☿) through an easy, free-flowing connection with the public (☊).

- Tele-evangelist Jim Bakker's unaspected Uranus is the Focal Point in the midpoint picture ♅ = ☉/♆, suggesting an individualistic expression (♅) through illuminated (☉) imagination or spirituality (♆). While this was probably the case early on with Bakker, a darker side of the same midpoint picture began to emerge. The individualistic expression deteriorated into self-misrepresentation and concealed issues (♆) that led to his imprisonment (♆) for fraud (♆). Again, remember that television is associated with Uranus.

- Johnny Carson's unaspected Uranus is the Focal Point in his midpoint picture ♅ = ☉/Mc, suggesting that individualistic expression (♅) can be accomplished through a definition of the ego (☉) through the career (Mc). Unaspected Uranus is also the Focal Point of the midpoint picture ♅ = ♂/♆, suggesting that his charisma (♂/♆) can help him in his quest for individualistic expression (♅).

Unaspected Neptune

When Neptune is unaspected, the individual must work particularly hard to confidently pursue his dreams and visions while avoiding disorienting influences. The challenge is to channel creative energies positively instead of gravitating toward delusions or escapism.

- Pianist Liberace's unaspected ♆ = ♃/♅ midpoint picture suggests that inspiration, escape, or fantasy needs (♆) can be accomplished through unrestrained (♃) individualistic expression (♅).

- Dutch artist Vincent Van Gogh's unaspected Neptune is the Focal Point of the ♆ = ♅/Asc midpoint picture. Van Gogh's midpoint picture vividly demonstrates the diverse extremes of interpretations that can be demonstrated in a single individual's life. Among the more positive interpretations of this midpoint picture is creativity (♆) that can be accomplished through embracing individualistic expression and personal (Asc) uniqueness (♅). While there is little dispute about Van Gogh's artistic creativity, a more challenging side of the same midpoint picture became a disruptive (♅) force in his personal (Asc) life. Personal (Asc) insecurities (♅) and feelings of being an outsider reinforce and allow the less productive Neptunian tendency toward disorientation and even delusional (♆) behavior.

- Walt Disney's unaspected Neptune is the Focal Point in his midpoint picture ♆ = ☿/♀, suggesting the pursuit of dreams or visions (♆) that can be accomplished by communicating thoughts and ideas (☿) beautifully and harmoniously (♀). Disney's dream began in earnest with Mickey Mouse's debut film in 1928, *Steamboat Willie*, the first animated (☿) cartoon (♀) with sound (☿).

Unaspected Pluto

When Pluto is unaspected, the individual must work particularly hard to channel his intensity into an empowerment to make dramatic, sweeping changes. The challenge is to recognize that sacrifices are often necessary to allow continued growth and progress.

- Sigmund Freud's unaspected Pluto is involved in the midpoint picture ♇ = ☉/☊, suggesting that empowerment, perspective, and transformation (♇) can be accomplished through an illuminated (☉) approach to others (☊).

- Vincent Van Gogh's ♇ = ☽/♆ midpoint picture involves his unaspected Pluto as the Focal Point. This picture suggests empowerment, perspective, and transformation (♇) that can be accomplished by nurturing emotional needs (☽) through idealism, dreams, or fantasy (♆). Van Gogh's impressionistic art possesses a dreamlike quality that encourages the viewer to *unfocus* his vision to fully appreciate the depth of perspective. This same midpoint picture also describes Van Gogh's difficult and tragic life, which was burdened by an intense (♇) struggle with his confused (♆) emotions (☽).

- The 14th Dalai Lama's unaspected Pluto is the Focal Point of the ♇ = ☿/♀ midpoint picture. This picture suggests empowerment, perspective, and transformation (♇) that can be accomplished through beautiful and harmonious (♀) thoughts, ideas, and communication (☿). He definitely has a way with words that powerfully (♇) provoke pleasant and peaceful (♀) thoughts (☿).

Note: By our definition, "unaspected" refers only to planets, and not to other points or celestial bodies. Therefore, no listings are included for the North Node, Ascendant, or Midheaven.

Another Technique for Analyzing Unaspected Planets

As mentioned previously in this section, when we find that the unaspected planet is not the Focal Point within orb of any midpoint pictures, we may choose to extend the orb from 2°00' to 2°30' from the Focal Point.

As an additional or alternative method to expanding the orb, we can examine midpoints in which an unaspected planet is represented in the midpoint (i.e., on the right-hand side of the midpoint picture equation). Using this alternative method, John Belushi's unaspected Uranus gives us these midpoint pictures:

$\mathical{D}$ = ♅/Mc   Emotional needs ($\mathical{D}$) can be accomplished through the public image (Mc) as eccentric or rebellious (♅) behavior.

☿ = ♅/♆   Efficient thoughts and communication (☿) can be accomplished through innovative (♅) dreams or visions (♆) or concealed (♆) eccentricity (♅).

Mc = ☿/♅   Career pursuits and public image (Mc) can be accomplished through innovative, unusual, or unconventional (♅) thoughts or ideas (☿).

The analysis of John Belushi's unaspected planets continues in the following discussion of multiple unaspected planets.

Multiple Unaspected Planets

When there are multiple unaspected planets, there may be a competition of sorts between the planets that are excluded from the intricate major-aspect structures that connect the other planets.

John Belushi has three unaspected plants: Sun, Saturn, and Uranus. As we examine Belushi's midpoints, we see two separate midpoint pictures that contain *two unaspected planets* at the midpoint (i.e., as components on the right-hand side of the midpoint picture equation).

♃ = ☉/♅   (Both the Sun and Uranus are unaspected.) This midpoint picture suggests that optimism and expansion—or excess (♃)—can be accomplished through an innovative (♅), illuminated (☉) expression of individuality (♅). John Belushi's off-the-wall performances so often seen on *Saturday Night Live* (particularly well demonstrated in the *SNL* news skits with Jane Curtin) illustrate this midpoint picture perfectly.

☊ = ♄/♅   The public appeal (☊) represented by Belushi's North Node in this mid-point picture also connects with two of his unaspected planets—Saturn and Uranus—and suggests his nonconformist, nontraditional (♅), rule-(♄) breaking (♅) image that endeared him to the public.

As a second example of multiple unaspected planets, Queen Elizabeth II's chart identifies no fewer than three unaspected planets. Interestingly, all three of her unaspected planets are *personal planets*—the Sun, Moon, and Mercury. On a personal level, this can be quite challenging. The life purpose or ego (☉), the emotional needs (☽), and the means of thinking and communicating efficiently (☿) are all challenged to gain integration with the rest of the planets and within the chart as a whole. As we attempt to gain additional insight, we can utilize any midpoint pictures in which the Focal Point represents one of these unaspected planets.

The Queen's Sun in Taurus is expected—by virtue of its sign placement—to be rather fixed, steady, and unwavering, reflecting a need to build and maintain security. As we bring in midpoint pictures related to the Sun, the plot thickens. *Ego definition and life purpose (☉) to build and maintain security (♉) can be accomplished through…*

☉ = ☿/Mc   *communication (☿) via a public forum (Mc).*

☉ = ☿/♄   *controlled, disciplined, focused (♄) thoughts, ideas, and communication (☿).*

☉ = ☽/☊   *nurturing emotional needs (☽) while working with or for others (☊).*

☉ = ☽/Asc   *nurturing emotional needs (☽) through introspection (Asc); setting an example.*

☉ = ♂/♇   *using energy (♂) for meaningful change (♇); promoting (♂) a new perspective (♇).*

Furthermore, the Queen's Moon in Leo identifies her need to be loved, respected, and honored. By studying midpoint pictures in which the Moon is the Focal Point, we can gain further insight. *Emotional needs (☽) and deserving respect, love, and honor (♌) can be accomplished through…*

☽ = ☉/♄   *an ambitious, determined, structured (♄) approach to life purpose (☉); a controlled, restrained (♄) ego (☉).*

$\mathbb{D} = \odot/\text{Mc}$ *an illuminated ($\odot$) public image (Mc).*

$\mathbb{D} = ♀/♀̆$ *a new social (♀) perspective (♀̆).*

Finally, unaspected Mercury in Aries *needs to communicate (☿) assertively and forcefully (♈) and can be accomplished through...*

$☿ = \mathbb{D}/\text{Mc}$ *a public display (Mc) of emotions ($\mathbb{D}$).*

$☿ = \mathbb{D}/♄$ *emotional ($\mathbb{D}$) reserve or restraint (♄).*

So which is it? These last two interpretations are contradictory, representing two radically different extremes of personal expression and communication. With these Mercury midpoint pictures suggesting either a public display of emotions or emotional reserve, the Queen is faced with (or blessed with) a choice. While we might initially see this potential range of expression as an inner conflict regarding how to best communicate, there is a deeper and more positive interpretation that incorporates both extremes.

For the Queen, being able to choose between these two midpoint pictures represents a tremendous amount of diversity (☿) within various avenues of communication (☿). Either influence can be tapped into, according to which style best fits the particular situation or the specific forum of communication. Situations requiring an emotional response can be handled just as easily as situations requiring more staid, unwavering, and unemotional communication. Whichever communication style is most appropriate for a specific venue is in her communication repertoire at all times.

Unlike John Belushi, Queen Elizabeth has no midpoint pictures that contain two unaspected planets as part of the midpoint (i.e., on the right-hand side of the equation).

Vincent Van Gogh's midpoint pictures are rather complicated, but quite interesting nonetheless. With *five* unaspected planets—the Sun, Saturn, Uranus, Neptune, and Pluto—his midpoint pictures lend significant insight into their interpretation.

$\odot = ♅/♆$ The unaspected Sun is the Focal Point in a midpoint picture that has two additional unaspected planets on the right side of the equation. This midpoint picture suggests that *the ego needs and the life purpose ($\odot$) can be accomplished through innovative (♅) or imaginative dreams or visions (♆). A less desirable interpretation suggests a clouded, veiled, or confused (♆) expression of individuality or eccentricity (♅).*

⛢ = ♄/♇   This midpoint picture also connects three of Van Gogh's unaspected planets—Uranus, Saturn, and Pluto—and suggests that *individualistic expression* (⛢) *can be accomplished through a monumental power struggle between traditional expectations* (♄) *and necessary, inevitable change* (♇).

Two unaspected planets show up in one of Hugh Hefner's midpoint pictures.

♆ = ♀/♂   This midpoint picture connects the unaspected Venus and Mars with Neptune as the Focal Point. This midpoint picture suggests that *inspiration or escape needs* (♆) *can be accomplished through use of energy* (♂) *for an aesthetic* (♀) *purpose, and also emphasizes an awareness of the male* (♂) *and female* (♀) *interaction, and sexual energy.* This vision (♆) led to Hefner's *Playboy* publication and allowed him to efficiently connect the energies of two unaspected planets, most appropriately Venus and Mars.

I have yet to run across a chart in which an unaspected planet is not represented either as the Focal Point of the midpoint picture or as a component of a midpoint, although this is not beyond the realm of possibility.

As you can see, there are multiple ways to use midpoints to gain insight into the previously elusive unaspected planets. It isn't necessary to consistently use *all* of these techniques, but it's quite helpful to have them at our disposal.

A Bit More on Orbs

When it comes to aspects and orbs, we have to know where to draw the line.

As a rule, when we look at any relationship between planets, the closer the relationship is to being exact, the more credibility we intuitively assign it. If an aspect is precise to the degree and minute, it logically merits more weight than does an aspect that is much further away, say 12°, from being exact.

This makes sense both intuitively and logically. One way to look at the closeness of an aspect is to consider an analogy to a magnet. When the magnet is adjacent to an object with the potential to be drawn to it (i.e., within orb), there can be no doubt about the attraction. To take this analogy to the point of absurdity, if the object is fifty miles away from the magnet, there is almost certainly no measurable, observable influence capable of drawing the object to the magnet.

The pertinent question then becomes, "At what point does the magnet no longer have an attractive influence on the object?" If you want to start a fight (or at least a heated argument) at a cocktail party for astrologers, bring up the question of orbs. You will probably hear about as many theories and techniques for determining orbs as there are astrologers in the room. It isn't really a question of who is right or wrong, but what works for each individual astrologer and what each considers to be reasonable.

Some astrologers, myself included, assign a slightly greater orb to the luminaries—the Sun and the Moon—than to the other planets or points. To go back to our magnet comparison, I assign the Sun and Moon "magnets" a slightly more powerful attractive influence.

So, bottom line, we each have to establish some sort of orb definition that we feel comfortable with. Otherwise, everything would aspect everything else and any meaningful analysis would be hopelessly mired in a murky swamp of not-too-important measurements.

As we discussed earlier, for the purposes of this book we assume an orb of 2° from the Focal Point for any midpoint picture to be considered. We could, as in the hypothetical astrologers' cocktail party above, argue this point *ad infinitum* (or at least *ad nauseam*) without making any appreciable headway. I recently—and accidentally—made a statement about aspects and orbs that some of my students considered rather profound. I said, "When it comes to aspects and orbs, we have to know where to draw the line." Regardless of your personal decision of what orbs to use in your natal or midpoint analysis, I encourage you to use them consistently but yet not adhere to them too obsessively, without any latitude of judgment.

For example, if you choose to use a 2° orb, you may find an occasional midpoint that is 2°01' away from a Focal Point. So, is it a cardinal (or perhaps fixed or mutable?) sin to include the associated midpoint picture? Of course it isn't. But such a midpoint almost certainly doesn't have the interpretive importance of a midpoint that is located much closer to that Focal Point.

Occasionally, I feel compelled to extend the orb just a bit when analyzing significant midpoint pictures that are slightly out of orb of a Focal Point. This would certainly include, but not be limited to, the supremely important ☉/☽ or Asc/Mc midpoints.

So when we see Eva Peron's Sun/Moon midpoint located just 2°02' away from her natal Pluto, I'd be hard-pressed not to include the ♇ = ☉/☽ midpoint picture in the analysis. This midpoint picture suggests *the potential for acquiring power and having a dramatic impact* (♇) *that can be accomplished through integration of ego* (☉) *and emotional needs* (☽). Her Sun in Taurus suggests the need for building security, while her Moon in Leo relishes and craves being the center of attention.

Another situation in which I don't hesitate to stretch the orb is when an unaspected planet has no midpoints that fall within a 2° orb. With unaspected planets, we are looking for clues to help us better understand how to integrate these planets into the whole chart. If that means slightly extending our previously carved-in-stone, unwavering 2° orb, then so be it.

As we discussed in the section on unaspected planets, John Belushi's Uranus has no Ptolemaic aspect within orb of another planet (i.e., it is unaspected). There are no midpoint pictures that fall within a 2° orb of Uranus, so we can look for a midpoint picture that is close to meeting our orb criteria. Upon further examination, we find that ♅ = ☿/☊ is just 2°03' away. The interpretation for this midpoint picture is *individualistic expression or innovation* (♅) *that can be accomplished through sharing thoughts and communication* (☿) *easily with the public* (☊). This midpoint picture offers a detailed clue as to how, through his eccentricity, Belushi was able to find and be embraced by such a willing audience.

The Closest Midpoint Picture

Okay. So now we have our orb ground rules firmly in mind.

Within each natal analysis, it is interesting and instructive to look at not only the closest *aspect* in the chart, but also the closest *midpoint picture*. This midpoint picture often identifies a dominant theme in the individual horoscope. How do we find the closest midpoint picture?

Using the 90° Midpoint Sort, we can calculate the difference between the Focal Points and the closest applicable midpoint for each. The single midpoint that comes closest to any Focal Point describes the midpoint picture that I'm referring to. This can be done with the 90° Sort, and it's just a matter of simple math, but it can be quite tedious. There is a much easier way, thanks to the computer.

If you use the 90° *Midpoint Tree* (in Win*Star, but other astrology programs should have a similar option), the midpoints are listed under each Focal Point with the closest midpoint listed first. Then it's just a matter of finding the single midpoint that comes closest to any of the Focal Points. When we examine the 90° Midpoint Tree (figure 9), we see that there are listings under each Focal Point with the corresponding midpoints and the distance separating the Focal Point from the midpoint, with the closest midpoint listed first. As we scan the first entry under each Focal Point, we simply locate the specific midpoint nearest to 00°00'. That combination of Focal Point and midpoint is our closest midpoint picture. It doesn't matter whether the midpoint is listed as a positive or a negative number, because we are concerned only with the relative distance separating the Focal Point from the midpoint, not whether it is applying or separating.

Referring to Sigmund Freud's 90° Midpoint Tree (figure 9), we begin our search with the listings under the Moon. We see that the closest listing in this section is 1°51' away from being exact. We then proceed to the listings below the Sun and find that the closest midpoint is within 0°13' of an exact match with the Sun. Next, we check the listings under Venus, Mars, etc., all the while keeping in mind the closest midpoint that we have encountered up to that time. We continue until the first listing under each Focal Point has been considered, at which time we will have determined the closest midpoint picture(s).

Again, referring to the example in figure 9, we find two midpoint pictures just 13' away from being exact.

When there is a tie for the closest midpoint picture, I look at each of these vying midpoint pictures equally, assigning an amplified—but equal—interpretive importance to each.

In the analysis of Freud's 90° Midpoint Tree, two midpoint pictures are equally close (within 13' of arc) to their respective Focal Points. The first, ☉ = ☿/♇, suggests that *the life purpose and identity definition* (☉) *can be accomplished through transformational* (♇) *thoughts, ideas, and communication* (☿). Alternatively, this same midpoint picture could suggest that the life purpose (☉) can be accomplished through a new perspective (♇) on the mind (☿). Freud said, "A man should not strive to eliminate his complexes but to get into accord with them: they are legitimately what directs his conduct in the world."[19]

The second midpoint picture that ties for the closest is ☊ = ♄/Mc, suggesting a relationship with the public (☊) that can be accomplished through using the career or the public image (Mc) to establish a solid foundation (♄).

Freud displayed ambivalence about the public perception of his work when he said, "What progress we are making. In the Middle Ages they would have burned me. Now they are content with burning my books."[20] It is interesting to note that burning for the pur-

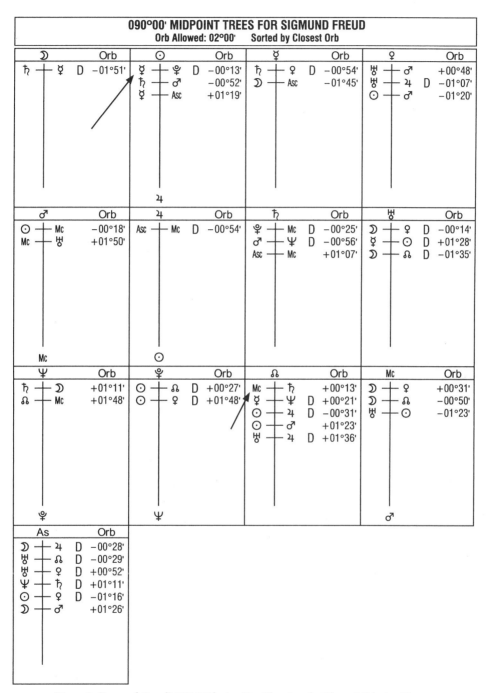

Figure 9. Sigmund Freud's 90° Midpoint Tree Showing the Closest Midpoint Pictures

pose of destroying is related to Pluto and books are associated with Mercury, another reference to the $\odot = \yen/\Psi$ midpoint picture, yet the Pluto component also describes the phoenix principle of rising from the ashes. Actually, Freud's quote may have been a little off base. In actuality, his life purpose ($\odot$) was to discard (Ψ) old beliefs about mental health ($\yen$) and to present the public (Ω) with the structure of a new foundation ($\hbar$) for analysis through his career (Mc), as represented by $\Omega = \hbar/Mc$, his other closest midpoint picture.

The Sun as the Focal Point in the Closest Midpoint Picture

- "Public Enemy Number One" John Dillinger has $\odot = \sigma/\jupiter$ as his closest midpoint picture, suggesting assertive (σ) growth, success ($\jupiter$), and over-the-top self-promotion. His ego needs ($\odot$) were stoked by his near cult status, which made him feel invincible. Although he sometimes used excessive ($\jupiter$) violence (σ), his reputation ($\odot$) was primarily due to his talent for robbing (σ) banks ($\jupiter$)!

- Goldie Hawn's closest midpoint picture, $\odot = \venus/\uranus$, suggests ego needs and identity definition ($\odot$) that can be accomplished through unconventional, unique, or unusual ($\uranus$) aesthetic beauty ($\venus$). Hawn's career got a major jumpstart on *Laugh-In*, the television show that featured her as an attractive ($\venus$) girl with a tendency toward spontaneous, uncontrolled ($\uranus$) giggling. Her unpredictable behavior made her delightfully appealing ($\venus$) in a rather unconventional ($\uranus$) way.

- Convicted Oklahoma City bomber Timothy McVeigh's closest midpoint picture is $\odot = \sigma/\saturn$. This picture suggests ego needs and identity definition ($\odot$) that can be accomplished through fierce (σ) determination ($\saturn$) to conquer obstacles. The darker side of this picture appears to have played out in McVeigh's life as frustrated ($\saturn$) energies (σ) in an attempt to define the ego or achieve the life purpose ($\odot$).

- Robin Williams has $\odot = \jupiter/\text{Asc}$ as his closest midpoint picture. This picture suggests that ego needs and identity definition ($\odot$) can be accomplished through trusting and showing off ($\jupiter$) personal abilities (Asc) and talents. Williams' manic ($\jupiter$) personality (Asc), uncensored spontaneity, and improvisational skills have become legendary.

The Moon as the Focal Point in the Closest Midpoint Picture

- Rock Hudson's closest midpoint picture of $\mathrm{D} = ♅/♆$ suggests emotional fulfillment needs (D) that can be accomplished through innovative (♅) or imaginative dreams or visions (♆). In reality, this midpoint picture also led him to conceal (♆) his nontraditional (♅) lifestyle.

- Tina Turner's $\mathrm{D} = ♀/♅$ suggests emotional needs (D) that can be accomplished through unconventional or unusual (♅) aesthetic beauty (♀), or social (♀) unrest or rebelliousness (♅). This influence in Turner's personal life emphasizes the volatile, unpredictable (♅) nature of love (♀), a sentiment well described in her megahit "What's Love Got to Do with It?"

- Oprah Winfrey's emotional fulfillment needs (D) can be accomplished through expansive (♃) career pursuits and public image (Mc), as represented by her closest midpoint picture of $\mathrm{D} = ♃/Mc$.

- Liberace's closest midpoint picture is $\mathrm{D} = ♂/♃$. Emotional fulfillment needs (D) can be accomplished through energetic (♂) growth and expansion (♃), over-the-top self-promotion, and flamboyance.

Mercury as the Focal Point in the Closest Midpoint Picture

- One of my personal favorites among the closest midpoint pictures is for LSD guru Timothy Leary. His closest midpoint picture, ☿ = ♅/♆, could be interpreted as efficient thoughts and communication (☿) that can be accomplished through nonconformist (♅) visions (♆). It isn't much of a stretch to apply this same midpoint picture to his admonition to "turn on (♆), tune in (☿), and drop out (♅)."[21]

- Aretha Franklin, "the Queen of Soul," has ☿ = ♂/♃ as her closest midpoint picture. This suggests that efficient thoughts and communication (☿) can be accomplished through energetic (♂) optimism and strength of conviction (♃). Also, perhaps she is asking (☿)—or demanding (♂)—to be given some "Respect" (♃).

- Jesse Jackson's closest midpoint picture is ☿ = ♃/♆, which suggests that efficient thoughts and communication (☿) can be accomplished through expansive, unrestricted (♃) visions (♆). This picture fits perfectly with his role as a spiritual (♆) minister (♃).

- Cult leader Charles Manson's closest midpoint picture is ☿ = ♃/♅. This suggests that efficient thoughts and communication (☿) can be accomplished through unrestrained (♃) individualistic expression (♅) or a devil-may-care attitude. In Manson's case, the potential for Jupiter's excessiveness combines with a Uranian recklessness taken to a horrifying extreme. The unrestrained (♃) chaos (♅) and disorderly confusion, suggested by one of the more unproductive manifestations of ♃/♅, could reasonably be called *Helter Skelter*. Fittingly, that is the title of the chilling biographical book documenting the Manson murders and the subsequent trial.

Venus as the Focal Point in the Closest Midpoint Picture

- Marilyn Monroe's closest midpoint picture of ♀ = ☿/♂ has Venus as the Focal Point. This midpoint picture suggests that social, aesthetic, or relationship (♀) needs can be accomplished through energetic or forceful (♂) thoughts and communication (☿). Monroe exhibited exceptional beauty (♀) that, combined with energetic and provocative (♂) communication skills (☿), helped propel her to Hollywood stardom.

- Another celebrity example with Venus as the Focal Point of the closest midpoint picture is Andy Warhol. His midpoint picture ♀ = ♄/Mc describes this underground artist (♀) who built a solid, stable (♄) career (Mc) through hard work, notably using plain, ordinary (♄) items such as the Campbell's Soup can.

- Dr. Phil McGraw, the popular television psychologist who got his big break on Oprah Winfrey's talk show, has ♀ = ♆/Mc as his closest midpoint picture. This picture suggests that social, aesthetic, or relationship (♀) needs can be accomplished through inspiration or creative visualization (♆) in the career (Mc). Dr. Phil has learned how to get through to people by helping them to creatively visualize their social situations rather than being confused or disoriented by their lives. The title of his number-one bestseller is *Self Matters: Creating Your Life from the Inside Out.*

Mars as the Focal Point in the Closest Midpoint Picture

- Mohandas Gandhi's closest midpoint picture is ♂ = ♀/♃. This suggests that efficient use of energy (♂) can be accomplished through social (♀) conviction (♃) and the use of his energy (♂) for peace (♀) and justice (♃).

- Branch Davidian leader David Koresh has ♂ = ♇/Asc, suggesting that efficient use of energy (♂) can be accomplished through self-empowerment, individual perspective, and transformation (♇) of self (Asc). This take-charge attitude can also relate to an evolutionary or revolutionary self-image.

- Mass murderer John Wayne Gacy's ♂ = ♀/♆ suggests that efficient energy use (♂) can be accomplished through social (♀) idealism (♆), but could also be interpreted as aggression (♂) through a confused vision (♆) of social (♀) norms or as socially (♀) deceptive (♆) actions (♂). Remember that Gacy used a clown (♀) costume (♆) in an attempt to disguise his motives (♂).

- John Hinckley, the would-be presidential assassin, has two exact midpoint pictures. The first, ♂ = ☉/♃, suggests using his energy (♂) in an enthusiastic (♃)—and in Hinckley's case, decidedly unrealistic—attempt to expand (♃) his ego (☉). (The other is listed under the North Node.)

- Johnny Carson's closest midpoint picture is ♂ = ☿/♅, suggesting that the efficient use of energy (♂) can be accomplished through innovative, unusual, or unconventional (♅) thoughts, ideas, and communication (☿). Carson's uncanny quick (♅) wit (☿) made him a late-night staple on *The Tonight Show* for more than thirty years.

Jupiter as the Focal Point in the Closest Midpoint Picture

- William Shatner's closest midpoint picture is ♃ = ☿/♅, suggesting that optimism, expansion, and rewards (♃) can be accomplished through innovative or unusual (♅) thoughts, ideas, or communication (☿). Shatner's role as Captain Kirk—the commander of the Starship Enterprise—received recognition and rewards (♃) for the long-running television series *Star* (♅) *Trek* (☿).

- Early rock pianist-vocalist Jerry Lee Lewis's closest midpoint picture is ♃ = ♀/Asc, suggesting optimism, expansion, and rewards (♃)—and possible excesses—that can be accomplished through personal (Asc) aesthetic, social, or relationship (♀) pursuits. Lewis's musical prowess led to a meteoric rise to stardom, but his career was dealt a serious setback when he married his thirteen-year-old cousin.

- Writer Henry Miller's ♃ = ☽/Mc midpoint picture features Jupiter at the Focal Point. This midpoint picture suggests optimism, expansion, and rewards (♃)—and also possible excesses—that can be accomplished by nurturing emotional needs (☽) through the career (Mc) or through a public display (Mc) of emotions (☽). In the cultural milieu when his books were published, Miller's emotionally charged literary works were considered obscene due to their erotic content.

Saturn as the Focal Point in the Closest Midpoint Picture

- Author Truman Capote's closest midpoint picture is ♄ = ☉/Mc, suggesting that necessary controls, structure, and stability (♄) can be accomplished by defining the ego (☉) through the career (Mc), by wanting public acclaim, and by thriving on the spotlight. Capote definitely loved the spotlight, although his public appearances did less to showcase his talent than to expose his personal vulnerabilities, such as his drug and alcohol problems.

- ♄ = ☉/Mc is also Béla Lugosi's closest midpoint picture. This picture suggests that necessary controls, structure, and stability (♄) can be accomplished through use of the career (Mc) to define the ego (☉), or by thriving in the spotlight. It is rather ironic that Lugosi's primary fame and reputation came as a result of his role in *Dracula*, the "Prince of Darkness," who hardly would have been comfortable in any sort of bright light.

- Muhammad Ali used his closest midpoint picture of ♄ = ☉/☊ to bring about stability (♄) through public exposure and his tremendous personal (☉) popularity with the public (☊). (A second midpoint picture that ties for Ali's closest is listed under the Midheaven).

- Author Stephen King's closest midpoint picture is ♄ = ♅/♆. This picture suggests that necessary controls, structure, and stability (♄) can be accomplished by innovative or imaginative (♅) dreams or visions (♆). King's unparalleled stature as a captivating storyteller comes from his unique ability to blend fantasy (♆) and the bizarre (♅).

Uranus as the Focal Point in the Closest Midpoint Picture

- ♅ = ☿/Asc is Howard Cosell's closest midpoint picture, suggesting that the potential route to individualistic expression (♅) was through the use of thoughts and communication (☿) to define himself (Asc).

- Baseball legend Jackie Robinson's Uranus is the Focal Point of his closest midpoint picture, ♅ = ♀/♄, and suggests that individualistic expression (♅) can be accomplished through social (♀) caution or reserve (♄). Before he became the first black player to enter baseball's major league, Robinson assured management that he would exercise restraint against the inevitable taunts, threats, and racial epithets to which he knew he would be subjected. Robinson kept his word, and performed far beyond all expectations in the process. What had at the time been a radical experiment (♅) succeeded in building a strong foundation (♄) for the reform of racial and social (♀) attitudes in professional sports and in society as a whole.

- Rush Limbaugh is certainly no stranger to individualistic expression, as we have come to associate this definition with Uranus at the Focal Point. Limbaugh's closest midpoint picture is ♅ = ♂/Mc, suggesting an energetic (♂) pursuit of career (Mc), and public self-promotion as a means of this individualistic expression (♅). Limbaugh's popular talk radio (♅) program is a high-powered vehicle for him to express and assert (♂) himself publicly (Mc).

Neptune as the Focal Point in the Closest Midpoint Picture

- For George Lucas, the closest midpoint picture is $\Psi = \sigma/\!\!\!\!\!\!\ast$, suggesting that inspiration or escape needs (Ψ) can be accomplished through energetically (σ) promoting innovation ($\!\!\!\!\!\!\ast$). Neptune is associated with film, Mars with conflict, and Uranus with astronomy, so $\Psi = \sigma/\!\!\!\!\!\!\ast$ could also mean a film—*Star Wars*.

- Versatile actor Dustin Hoffman has $\Psi = \varphi/\sigma$ as his closest midpoint picture. This picture suggests that inspiration or escape needs can be accomplished through energy (σ) use for an aesthetic (φ) purpose and an awareness of male-female principles. His role in the film *Tootsie* offered a vehicle that cinematically allowed him to explore different treatments of the genders in a comedic way, while still making a point. This midpoint picture also appropriately describes the sexually disorienting and confusing situations encountered in *The Graduate*.

- Amelia Earhart has $\Psi = \hbar/\text{Mc}$ as the closest midpoint picture, suggesting that inspiration or escape needs (Ψ) can be met by career (Mc) determination ($\hbar$), and by being one's own boss or by being in control. It is interesting that she was known for her solo ($\hbar$) flights, an expression of her self-reliance, and also for being in charge and totally responsible ($\hbar$) for herself. The ultimate irony of this midpoint picture is her mysterious (Ψ) disappearance during a highly publicized (Mc), determined, and ambitious ($\hbar$) attempt to fly around the world.

Pluto as the Focal Point in the Closest Midpoint Picture

- For Jim Henson, the closest midpoint picture is ♇ = ♂/☊, suggesting that dramatic, sweeping changes (♇) can be accomplished through working energetically (♂) with the public (☊). His amazing success and the resultant impact—particularly on young children—belies his modest self-appraisal when he said, "My hope still is to leave the world a bit better than when I got here."[22]

- Napoleon's closest midpoint picture, ♇ = ♂/♃, accurately describes his motivation to change the world in big ways (♇) that can be accomplished through energetic (♂) optimism (♃) and feeling invincible. Napoleon said, "Great ambition is the passion of a great character."[23]

- Joan Crawford's closest midpoint picture of ♇ = ☽/♀ reflects her idealistic social (♀) and emotional (☽) perspective (♇). She said, "I have always known what I wanted, and that was beauty... in every form."[24] Her alleged tyrannical (♇) treatment of her adoptive daughter, Christine, was suggested in the biographical movie *Mommie* (☽) *Dearest* (♀)!

- Adolf Hitler's closest midpoint picture perfectly describes his personal ambition. With ♇ = ☉/♃, empowerment, perspective, and transformation (♇) are suggested, with a focus on power (♇) that can be accomplished through enthusiastic goals (♃), self-aggrandizement, or an inflated (♃) ego (☉). It isn't much of a stretch to see how this midpoint picture could be interpreted as belonging to an egomaniacal (☉/♃) dictator (♇).

The North Node as the Focal Point in the Closest Midpoint Picture

- César Chavez's ☊ = ♂/♇ suggests that his relationship with the public (☊) can be accomplished through promoting (♂) a new perspective (♇) and provoking (♂) a major change (♇). Much of Chavez's energy was focused specifically on the plight of migrant farm workers.

- One of the two exact midpoint pictures for would-be presidential assassin John Hinckley is ☊ = ♃/Mc (the other is listed previously under Mars), suggesting that his relationship with the public (☊) can be accomplished through seeking or expecting public (Mc) rewards or recognition (♃) for his accomplishments. Although his attack did indeed bring him a degree of recognition in the form of notoriety, it certainly did not bring about the public admiration to which he had aspired.

- John DeLorean's closest midpoint picture of ☊ = ♅/♇ suggests a relationship with the public (☊) that can be accomplished through big changes (♇) for innovation (♅). DeLorean's life was a frenzy (♅) of new beginnings (♇), including three marriages that ended in divorce (♅). In his professional life, after rising to the pinnacle of management at General Motors (automobiles = ♅), he chucked it all and began his own DeLorean Motor Company. When the car company encountered financial hardships, chaos (♅) ensued when he was involved in a major destructive (♇) drug scandal, and although he denied any personal cocaine use, the disruptive upheaval resulted in irreparable damage to his public image.

The Ascendant as the Focal Point in the Closest Midpoint Picture

- For John Lennon, with his closest midpoint picture of ASC = ♃/♆, identity definition (ASC) can be accomplished through expansive (♃), creative visualization (♆). Remember that in an earlier section we mentioned one of his biggest hits, "Imagine," in which he says, "Imagine all the people living life in peace. You may say I'm a dreamer, but I'm not the only one."

- Guyana cult leader Jim Jones's closest midpoint picture of ASC = ☉/♂ reflects his potential for public projection and identity definition (ASC) through assertive self-promotion (☉/♂).

- Rocker Janis Joplin's closest midpoint picture of ASC = ♃/♆ sets the stage for an identity (ASC) defined by expansive, unrestricted (♃) visions and dreams (♆), but also sends up a red flag suggesting the possibility of excessive (♃) escapism (♆).

The Midheaven as the Focal Point in the Closest Midpoint Picture

- Tele-evangelist Jim Bakker's closest midpoint picture is MC = ♂/ASC. This suggests that the career pursuits and a public image (MC) can be accomplished through energetic (♂) self-promotion (♂/ASC).

- Evangelist Billy Graham's closest midpoint picture is MC = ☽/♇ and is exact at 00°00'. This suggests that his public image and his career pursuits (MC) can be accomplished through nurturing emotional needs (☽) through empowerment, perspective, and transformation (♇). Graham's emotional (☽) and passionate intensity (♇) powerfully defines his public persona (MC).

- Mae West's effusive public persona is shown vividly in her closest midpoint picture, MC = ♃/☊. Her career (MC) was the perfect vehicle for her gregarious personal style and propelled her to public (☊) success (♃) and popularity.

- Muhammad Ali's MC = ♀/ASC midpoint picture ties for the closest in his chart (the other is listed under Saturn). This midpoint picture suggests the self- (ASC) empowerment (♀) that some interpreted as arrogance or aloofness, as well as his well-publicized (MC) personal (ASC) conversion (♀) to Islam.

The Aries Point

There is an especially efficient conduit that links the inner workings of the individual's horoscope to the external world.

The portal for this connection clearly involves the Aries Point.

The Aries Point Defined

I was initially exposed to Aries Point terminology in Noel Tyl's *Synthesis & Counseling in Astrology.* As I began looking for additional references, it quickly became obvious that very few modern texts devote much, if any, attention to the Aries Point (AP). Notable exceptions are Robert Hand's *Horoscope Symbols* and several of Noel Tyl's other books that include references to the AP.

Actually, the term Aries Point is somewhat of a misnomer. The Aries Point is technically defined as 0° Aries on the zodiac wheel; however, the more commonly and widely accepted Aries Point definition refers to 0° of *all the cardinal signs* (♈, ♋, ♎, and ♑). Another way to look at it is that we include not only the 0° Aries location, but also all points in opposition or square to this point, leaving us with the four positions at 0° of each point of the Cardinal Grand Cross.

These placements located near the early degrees of the cardinal signs have long been associated with initiation, getting things rolling, and people who are "movers and shakers."

The suggested orb is 2° on either side of 0° of all cardinal signs. Using this orb (as seen in figure 10), we find that the defined AP range spans locations from 28°00' of any mutable sign to 2°00' of the *adjacent* cardinal sign.[25]

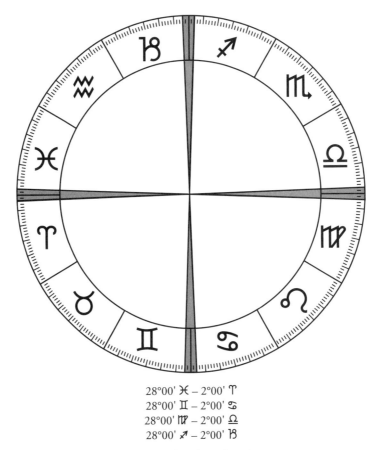

28°00' ♓ – 2°00' ♈
28°00' ♊ – 2°00' ♋
28°00' ♍ – 2°00' ♎
28°00' ♐ – 2°00' ♑

Figure 10. Aries Point Locations

Incorporating the Aries Point into chart interpretation often proves to be quite en-lightening, as it suggests the direction of public endeavors related to any planet, point, or midpoint that is in contact with the AP.

Although the area associated with the Aries Point represents a relatively small segment when compared to the chart as a whole (less than 4.5 percent of all possible placements when using a 2° orb), this location is exquisitely sensitive in its interpretive connection with public projection potential. These small areas of the chart represent veritable hotbeds for the germination and growth of our potential for public projection and suggest a spe-cific direction for the externalized focus of the individual.

While traditional natal chart interpretation focuses primarily on personal traits and characteristics, incorporating the Aries Point allows us to extend the focus beyond the individual and suggests a template for connection to the outside world.

Contact with the Aries Point helps to characterize the potential for the individual's ability to efficiently relate to the outside world, and represents the potential for public projection related to any Focal Point (or midpoint) that is located within this region.

However, merely having contact with the Aries Point is by no means an ironclad, double-your-money-back guarantee of fame and fortune. **It is crucial to remember that the horoscope as a whole suggests the *potential* of the individual, rather than a specific, absolutely predetermined outcome.** We must also recognize that residing within this anticipated potential lies a relatively wide latitude of expression for any given contact. As discussed in chapter 2 regarding polarities, **there is always potentially a more positive and a less positive manifestation for any specific measurement.** As we will see in some examples, there may have been situations in which individuals would rather not have been identified with and remembered for their specific manifestation of the Aries Point contact.

As my study of the AP has continued over the years, I have been astonished to note the validity of the insight contributed by incorporating this relatively infrequently used measurement. Thanks in large part to the tremendous compilation of reliable astrological birth data by Lois Rodden and Mark McDonough of AstroDatabank™, it has been possible to assemble some illuminating examples of the Aries Point in the charts of celebrities and prominent, well-known people. Continuing research has produced stacks of examples that vividly demonstrate how the AP can be an accurate indicator of an individual's "potential for public projection." Often this measurement is uncannily related to the person's claim to fame or what he will be remembered for.

Identifying the Aries Point Region Using the 90° Midpoint Sort

With a little practice, Aries Point contact can easily be identified and its inclusion can add a fascinating dimension to the overall natal chart analysis. The 90° Midpoint Sort table is particularly helpful, as it allows the astrologer to quickly identify the applicable Focal Point(s) or midpoint(s) associated with the AP. Any Focal Point or midpoint within the established 2° orb of the AP will show up in the 90° Sort in either the 0°–2°00' range (corresponding to 0°–2°00' of any cardinal signs) or in the 88°–89°59' of the sort (corresponding to 28°–29°59' of any mutable sign placement).

Referring again to Jim Henson's 90° Midpoint Sort (figure 11), we see that two individual Focal Points fall within the Aries Point range, including the Sun at 1°01' (corresponding to 1°01' of a cardinal sign) and the North Node at 88°46' (corresponding to 28°46' of a mutable sign). By virtue of their proximity to the 0° AP location, we know that these two points (the Sun and the North Node) must be either conjunct, square, or in opposition to one another in the natal chart. In Jim Henson's case, the Sun is square the North Node, but as we've already learned, their proximity in the 90° Sort suggests the *tension* between the two, and this tension is more significant than the nature of the specific aspect.

Jim Henson *Sep 24, 1936* *12:10:00 AM CST* *091W03'00"* *33N24'00"*

Midpoint Sort: 90° Dial

☿/♆	000°43'	☉/♀	012°44'	♂/☊	028°39'	☊/Mc	046°45'	☉/♇	059°45'	♄	078°12'
☉	001°01'	♅/♆	013°01'	☽/♂	031°41'	♆/Asc	047°44'	☿/Asc	061°23'	♅/♇	078°44'
☿/♄	001°17'	♄/♅	013°35'	♀/♅	031°42'	☽/☉	047°55'	♇/Mc	061°37'	☿/♂	081°27'
☽/☊	001°48'	♇/☊	013°38'	♃/♆	032°13'	♄/Asc	048°18'	♅/☊	063°52'	♃/☊	083°05'
☉/Mc	002°52'	☿	014°22'	♃/♄	032°48'	☽/Mc	049°47'	♀/Asc	066°26'	☉/♆	084°02'
♃/Asc	002°54'	♀/Mc	014°35'	♆/☊	037°55'	♀/♃	050°55'	☿/♇	066°26'	☉/♄	084°36'
♂/♅	003°45'	☽/♇	016°40'	♂/Asc	038°28'	☿/☊	051°34'	☽/♅	066°54'	♆/Mc	085°54'
Mc	004°44'	Asc	018°25'	♄/☊	038°29'	♆/♇	052°46'	♂/♆	067°47'	☽/♃	086°07'
☽	004°50'	☿/♀	019°24'	♅	038°58'	♄/♇	053°21'	♂/♄	068°22'	♄/Mc	086°28'
♀/♆	005°45'	☉/♅	019°59'	☉/♃	039°12'	☽/☿	054°36'	♀/♇	071°28'	♀/♂	086°29'
♀/♄	006°19'	♅/Mc	021°51'	☽/♆	040°57'	☉/Asc	054°43'	♅/Asc	073°41'	☊	088°46'
☉/☿	007°41'	♂/♃	022°57'	♃/Mc	041°04'	Mc/Asc	056°35'	☉/♂	074°46'		
♃/♇	007°56'	♇/Asc	023°27'	☽/♄	041°31'	♀/☊	056°36'	♂/Mc	076°38'		
☊/Asc	008°35'	♀	024°26'	♂/♇	043°30'	♃/♅	058°11'	♆	077°04'		
☿/Mc	009°33'	☿/♅	026°40'	☉/☊	044°53'	♂	058°31'	♃	077°23'		
☽/Asc	011°37'	♇	028°29'	☿/♃	045°53'	☽/♀	059°38'	♄/♆	077°38'		

0°00'–2°00' = Cardinal Sign Placement (♈ ♋ ♎ ♑)
88°00'–89°59' = Mutable Sign Placement (♊ ♍ ♐ ♓)

Figure 11. Using the 90° Midpoint Sort to Identify Aries Point Midpoints and Midpoint Pictures

When the **Aries Point** is the Focal Point of a midpoint picture,
it suggests the *potential for public projection...*

AP =

⊙   to become well-known; ego energy is expended to gain notice or stature.

☽   by connecting emotionally with the public; by nurturing, protecting, or provoking an emotional response.

☿   through communication, writing, ideas, or other intellectual activities.

♀   through anything pleasing to the senses, such as art, music, or physical beauty; through activities in the social arena.

♂   of aggression, courage, drive, ruggedness, sexuality, or athleticism.

♃   of success, wealth, optimism, enthusiasm, expansion, or generosity—or through excessive behavior.

♄   through the public image as ambitious, reliable, disciplined, self-sufficient, or under control.

♅   through individualistic expression; through innovation, rebelliousness, or eccentricity.

♆   through an idealistic pursuit as a visionary, spiritual leader, or dreamer; or for confused, dishonest, or deceptive behavior.

♇   as a pioneer or as a reformer for dramatic, sweeping change; or through involvement in secretive or subversive behavior.

☊   of an ability to easily connect with groups or with the public in general.

Asc   of an ability to easily gain public popularity; by having congenial personality traits conducive to public attraction.

Mc   to easily utilize the career or public image to attract public attention and exposure.

Figure 12. Interpretation Guidelines for Focal Points at the Aries Point

As in Jim Henson's chart, in which there is at least one Focal Point within the orb of the Aries Point, we have a starting point for our analysis of how the potential for public projection will likely present itself in the individual's life (see figure 12). When there is a Focal Point within the AP range, our equation reads:

AP = Focal Point

Using only the interpretations associated with the two specific Focal Points within the orb of the Aries Point in Jim Henson's chart *without the associated midpoints*, we could say that:

AP = ☉   *There is a potential for public projection to become well-known; ego energy is expended to gain notice or stature.*

AP = ☊   *There is a potential for public projection of an ability to easily connect with groups or with the public in general.*

Although these two Focal Points located within the Aries Point region go a long way to describe the potential for public projection, even more interpretive insight and specificity are possible by incorporating midpoints to create Aries Point midpoint pictures.

Incorporating Midpoint Pictures With the AP

When there is direct contact between a specific Focal Point and the AP (within a 2° orb), there is frequently a profound relationship in which the energies traditionally associated with that particular planet are *publicly demonstrated* by the individual.

When there is a midpoint associated with the Focal Point in the AP region, we simply add another equals sign to our equation:

AP = Focal Point = Planet or Point #1/Planet or Point #2

With Jim Henson's Sun at 1°01', we look for midpoints in the range of 89°01' to 3°01'.

For his North Node at 88°46', we look for midpoints between 86°46' and 0°46' (which is equivalent to 90°46' in the 90° Midpoint Sort format).

We can then construct the following midpoint pictures and their respective interpretations by beginning each statement with the standard Aries Point preface: *There is a potential for public projection…*

AP = ☉ = ☿/♆	to become well-known; ego energy is expended to gain notice or stature (AP = ☉). This can be accomplished through imaginative (♆) thoughts, ideas, and communication (☿).
AP = ☉ = ☿/♄	to become well-known; ego energy is expended to gain notice or stature (AP = ☉). This can be accomplished through creating reality (♄) from thoughts or ideas (☿) and putting them into a tangible (♄) form.
AP = ☉ = ☽/☊	to become well-known; ego energy is expended to gain notice or stature (AP = ☉). This can be accomplished through nurturing emotional needs (☽), or making contact and working with or for others (☊).
(AP = ☉ = ♃/Asc)[26]	to become well-known; ego energy is expended to gain notice or stature (AP = ☉). This can be accomplished through trusting and showing off (♃) one's personal (Asc) abilities and talents.
AP = ☊ = ☿/♆	of an ability to easily connect with groups or with the public in general (AP = ☊). This can be accomplished through imaginative (♆) thoughts, ideas, and communication (☿).

It quickly becomes apparent that there often will be considerable repetition contained within these individual interpretations. We can simplify the shorthand to further consolidate midpoint pictures into one or two multifaceted equations. From our example above, we could summarize all the applicable information with just two lines of equations:

AP = ☉ = ☿/♆ = ☿/♄ = ☽/☊ (= ♃/Asc)

AP = ☊ = ☿/♆

Note that we cannot combine the Sun and North Node focal points into the same midpoint picture equation because only the ☿/♆ midpoint is shared by both Focal Points.

Interpretively, this format triggers our memories to associate specific keywords with the equations. By doing so, it is easier to merge their combined suggested meanings into more concise statements. For this example, we could distill our thoughts by stating:

There is a potential for public projection (AP) by using energy for ego recognition (☉) and by an ability to easily connect with groups or with the public in general (☊). This can be accomplished by working with others to emotionally (☽) communicate (☿) imaginative thoughts, visions (♆), and ideas (☿) and put them into tangible form (♄).

As you can see, it becomes less important to follow strict interpretive guidelines than to incorporate significant concepts into a few meaningful and easily understood sentences.

As we continue the Aries Point interpretations, we will examine each of the planets and points and discuss the suggested meaning when each makes natal contact with the Aries Point, particularly as the Focal Point.

☉ contact with the AP—*suggests the potential for public projection to become well-known: ego energy is expended to gain notice or stature.*

- Actress Meryl Streep has the midpoint picture AP = ☉ = ☽/♇. This picture suggests the potential for public projection and definition of ego (AP = ☉) that can be accomplished through the intensity (♇) of emotions (☽) or by needing to make a dramatic difference through the use of emotions. One of the most respected actresses in Hollywood, Streep has received fourteen Oscar nominations.

- Famed mime Marcel Marceau has the midpoint picture AP = ☉ = ☿/♄, which suggests the potential for public projection and ego definition (AP = ☉) that can be accomplished through giving structure or substance (♄) to thoughts and ideas (☿). Marceau became known for (AP) and identified with (☉) his rather unique method of silent (♄) communication (☿).

- Author James Redfield has the AP = ☉ = ♄/♆ midpoint picture. This picture suggests the potential for public projection (AP) and definition of ego (☉) that can be accomplished through giving substance (♄) to the dream (♆) or making the intangible (♆) tangible (♄). Redfield's self-published *The Celestine Prophecy* became a bestseller and gave his readers an inspirational look at spirituality. The book also eventually led to a sequel, *The Celestine Vision* (♆).

☽ contact with the AP—suggests the potential for public projection through an emotional connection with the public: by nurturing, protecting, or provoking an emotional response.

- The Italian-French sculptor Frédéric-Auguste Bartholdi has his natal Moon at the Aries Point, which represents the Focal Point in the midpoint picture AP = ☽ = ♀/♆. The suggestion from this midpoint picture is an emotional connection (☽) with the public that can be accomplished through an aesthetic or social (♀) transformation or new perspective (♆). Bartholdi designed and built the Statue of Liberty as a gift from France to the American people. One can only imagine the emotional (☽) responses from the countless immigrants coming into New York Harbor looking for equality (♀) and a new start (♆).

- Lech Walesa, the Polish labor leader, has his Moon at the Aries Point in the midpoint picture AP = ☽ = ♇/Mc. This picture suggests the potential for public projection (AP) and an emotional connection (☽) with the public that can be accomplished through a highly visible (Mc) empowerment, perspective, and transformation for dramatic change (♇).

- Deepak Chopra's AP = ☽ = ☿/♄ midpoint picture suggests the potential for public projection (AP) to connect emotionally (☽) that can be accomplished through a creation of reality (♄) from thoughts, ideas, and communication (☿). This concept is perfectly illustrated by the title of his book *Mastering the Forces That Shape Personal Reality.*

☿ *contact with the AP—suggests the potential for public projection through communication, writing, ideas, and intellectual activities.*

- Louis Pasteur has AP = ☿ = ♃/Mc, suggesting a potential for public projection of thoughts, ideas, and communication (AP = ☿) that can be accomplished through expansive (♃) public pursuits (Mc). Although Pasteur's major accomplishments may be better known, it is interesting to note that "he put in place an exceedingly modern education concept by offering evening classes for the workmen of the city,"[27] effectively expanding (♃) educational (☿) opportunities for people to further themselves and their careers (Mc).

- The Hollywood gossip columnist Rona Barrett's Mercury at the Aries Point suggests that her potential for public projection would be related to communication (☿). With a midpoint picture of AP = ☿ = ☉/♆, we would expect such communication to be illumination (☉) of visions or perhaps of concealed issues (♆). It is interesting to note that Mercury has connotations with rumors and gossip and with columnists.

- Actor Sean Connery has the midpoint picture AP = ☿ = ♆/☊, suggesting the potential for public projection through communication, thoughts, or, ideas (☿) that can be accomplished through the use of dreams and visions (♆) to connect with the public (☊). Connery seemed to fit perfectly in his movie role as James Bond. In fact, many 007 aficionados consider Connery to be the quintessential spy (♆) James Bond.

♀ contact with the AP—suggests the potential for public projection through anything pleasing to the senses, such as art, music, or physical beauty; or through activities in the social arena.

- Athlete and actor O. J. Simpson's AP = ♀ = ☽/♆ suggests public acclaim for social or aesthetic (♀) venues that can be accomplished through emotional (☽) sensitivity (♆). The downside of this midpoint picture is the possibility of emotional (☽) confusion or disorientation (♆) in relationships (♀).

  Another of O. J.'s Aries Point midpoint pictures that features Venus at the Focal Point is AP = ♀ = ☿/♂. This suggests that the potential for public projection, aesthetically or socially (♀), can be accomplished through energetic, assertive, or forceful (♂) thoughts (☿)—or through possibly controversial, provocative, or argumentative actions or behavior.

- Sir Alexander Fleming's unaspected Venus is at the Aries Point. One of the resultant midpoint pictures, AP = ♀ = ☉/♆, suggests the potential for public projection of aesthetics or something with a social orientation (♀) that can be accomplished through an illuminated (☉) imagination (♆). Fleming will be best remembered (AP) for his Nobel Prize for medicine for the discovery of penicillin. His cure (♀) came from mold—a quite unlikely source—and brought to light an important (☉) new drug (♆) with an immeasurable benefit to society (♀).

- Lou Ferrigno's AP = ♀ = ♂/♄ suggests the potential for public projection through a social or aesthetic (♀) vehicle that can be accomplished through fierce (♂) determination (♄) to conquer (♂) obstacles (♄). To compensate for social frustration as a result of a severe hearing loss (♄) from infections (♂) early in life, Ferrigno began to build (♄) muscles (♂) and eventually became a competitive (♂) bodybuilder. His impressive physique led to Ferrigno being cast in the role of a superhero in *The Incredible Hulk*.

♂ contact with the AP—suggests the potential for public projection of aggression, courage, drive, ruggedness, sexuality, or athleticism.

- Midpoint pictures for the artist formerly (and currently) known as Prince reveal his Mars at the Aries Point. Not only is Mars unaspected, but it is also the Focal Point of the closest midpoint picture ♂ = ☽/☊ (exact at 0°00') and is in its own sign of Aries. All this Martian energy combines powerfully to suggest the potential for an energetic (♂) public projection that can be accomplished by nurturing an emotional (☽) need to connect with the public (☊).

    Prince's hyperactive Mars also forms the midpoint picture AP = ♂ = ♆/Mc, suggesting energy (♂) focused on an elusive, nebulous (♆) career or public image (Mc).

    Prince's Mars forms yet another midpoint picture, AP = ♂ = ♆/♇, suggesting that imagination and visions (♆) can yield dramatic outcomes (♇). Energy may be used to create the illusion (♆) of power (♇), or energy may be focused on sexual (♇) fantasy (♆).

- Even though we don't know Thomas Edison's birth time, there is no doubt that his AP = ♂ = ♀/♇ midpoint picture is correct. This picture suggests that the potential for public projection (AP) and efficient use of energy (♂) can be accomplished through an aesthetic or social (♀) transformation (♇). The new perspective ushered in by Edison was a result of his invention of not only the light bulb, but also the phonograph and motion pictures that served to redefine life's conveniences and pleasures.

- Steven Spielberg's AP = ♂ = ♆/Mc midpoint picture suggests a potential for public projection and an efficient use of energy (♂) that can be accomplished through a spiritual or inspirational (♆) career or public image (Mc). While Spielberg's talents as a motion picture (♆) producer and director are legendary, a spiritual theme was evident in his profoundly disturbing yet inspirational *Schindler's List*, which was voted best picture of the year in 1994 and earned him an Academy Award for his direction.

♃ *contact with the AP*—*suggests the potential for public projection of success, wealth, optimism, expansion, enthusiasm, or generosity—or through excessive behavior.*

- Sigmund Freud's AP = ♃ = Asc/Mc suggests that his potential for public projection was of an expansive (♃) nature, and in his case, it particularly related to the higher mind. As will be discussed later in this chapter in the section "Special AP Midpoint Pictures" (AP = Asc/Mc), this midpoint picture represents a link—a connection—between the public persona (Mc) and the more personal expression of identity (Asc).

- Presidential assassin Lee Harvey Oswald has AP = ♃ = ♂/♅. This midpoint picture suggests an expansive/excessive (♃) potential for public projection (AP) that can be accomplished through a restless, energetic drive (♂) toward individualistic expression (♅). This midpoint picture also can suggest unrestrained (♃), impulsive (♅) actions (♂) or taking reckless risks.

- M. C. Escher, the Dutch artist, has the midpoint picture AP = ♃ = ♀/☊, which suggests an expansive, unrestrained (♃) potential for public projection (AP) that can be accomplished through presenting the public (☊) with a new perspective (♀). Escher's unconventional etchings showed the public something to which it hadn't previously been exposed.

♄ contact with the AP—suggests the potential for public projection through the public image by being ambitious, reliable, disciplined, self-sufficient, or under control.

- Mae West, with her AP = ♄ = Asc/Mc = ☉/♅ = ♀/♆, would hardly be considered conservative, as part of our definition suggests. Despite being known for her suggestive, flirtatious, and sometimes borderline-outrageous behavior, she never crossed the line (remember that Saturn represents *necessary controls*). She always knew exactly how far she could push something and how much she could get away with. Her illuminated (☉) individuality (♅) and eccentric (♅) approach to life (☉) combine to create a sensual feeling and a harmonious (♀) vision (♆), so that with Mae, what you see is what you get (Asc/Mc).[28]

- David Koresh, the leader of the Branch Davidian cult in Waco, Texas, has the midpoint picture AP = ♄ = ☉/♆. This suggests the potential for public projection and necessary controls (♄) that can be accomplished through an illuminated (☉) imagination, dream, or spirituality (♆). It can also suggest maintaining control (♄) by public projection (AP) through a delusional or confused (♆) view of, or representation of, self (☉).

- Even though we don't know the birth time of J.R.R. Tolkien, author of the meticulously elaborate Middle Earth in *The Hobbit* and *The Lord of the Rings*, there is no doubt that he has both Saturn and Mercury represented as Focal Points of the midpoint picture AP = ☿ = ♄ = ♀/☊. While the combination of Mercury and Saturn at the AP suggests efficiently structured (♄) thoughts (☿) and disciplined (♄) communication (☿), the shared ♀/☊ midpoint adds an aesthetic attraction (♀) and public appeal (☊).

♅ *contact with the AP—suggests the potential for public projection through individualistic expression; through innovation, rebelliousness, or eccentricity.*

- Christine Jorgensen's AP = ♅ = ☿/Asc suggests an unusual, out-of-the-mainstream (♅) public projection through thoughts and communication (☿) that help to define the identity (Asc). Just imagine the unusual feelings that must have gone through his/her mind and the process of introspection (☿/Asc) prior to becoming one of the first—and certainly the most public at the time—to undergo a sex change operation.

- Marilyn Monroe's AP = ♅ = ☉/☊ midpoint picture describes the potential for public projection and a unique expression of identity (♅) that thrived and shined in the spotlight (☉) of public attention (☊) and exposure.

- With Uranus at the Aries Point and the midpoint picture of AP = ♅ = ☊/Mc, the suggestion is one of innovation or eccentricity (♅) that can be accomplished through the public image. This midpoint picture belongs to Salvador Dali, the Spanish painter with a flair for the bizarre (♅) in his public image (both ☊ and Mc) and in his surrealistic artistic creations. The photograph of Dali with wide, wild eyes and an elaborate moustache creates an image that many will always associate with him. A rebel and a nonconformist (♅), he often felt like an outcast, although his artistic work was nonetheless brilliant.

♆ *contact with the AP—suggests the potential for public projection through an idealistic pursuit as a visionary, spiritual leader, or dreamer; or for confused, dishonest, or deceptive behavior.*

- Muhammad Ali's AP = ♆ = ♅/♇ midpoint picture suggests that he might be remembered for being elusive (♆) both inside and outside of the ring. His public image (AP) was somewhat nebulous and confused (♆) due to his status as a conscientious objector (♅) during the Vietnam War, for which he forfeited his boxing title. The *dramatic change for rebirth* interpretation of the ♅/♇ midpoint parallels his religious (♆) conversion (♅) and name change from Cassius Clay to Muhammad Ali.

- Jesse Jackson has his Neptune at the Aries Point and also in the AP = ♆ = ☽/♇ midpoint picture. The potential for public projection relates to inspiration and visualization (♆) that can be accomplished through empowerment, a new perspective, and transformation or by making a powerful change (♇) through the use of emotions (☽). This midpoint picture is apparent in the Reverend Jackson's work as a minister and in his political and social pursuits. Another side of this midpoint picture relates to his 2001 admission of an extramarital affair, which brings into play the hidden, concealed association of Neptune. With Neptune at the Aries Point, however, it is likely that any attempts to conceal facts will not be successful; they eventually will be brought out in public. The ☽/♇ midpoint further defines this event as an intensity (♇) of emotions (☽) resulting from the attempted concealment (♆).

- Lest we think that these definitions apply only to contemporary individuals, consider that Renaissance man Leonardo da Vinci also has Neptune at the Aries Point (within 0°01' of being exact). His AP = ♆ = ♀/♅ suggests a potential for public projection through a visionary (♆) approach used to accomplish aesthetic (♀) innovation (♅), perhaps with some social (♀) rebelliousness or idiosyncrasies (♅) thrown in for good measure.

And we would be remiss if we ignored the darker side of Neptune.

- Mass murderer Richard Speck's AP = ♆ = ♄/♇ suggests the potential for public projection of confusion, fantasy, or camouflage (♆) by taking control (♄) over life and death (♇).

Ironically, another mass murderer, John Wayne Gacy, has the same AP = ♆ = ♄/♇ midpoint picture.

♇ *contact with the AP—suggests the potential for public power as a pioneer or as a reformer for dramatic, sweeping change; or involvement in secretive or subversive behavior.*

- Louis Pasteur's AP = ♇ = ♃/Mc suggests the potential for public projection that involves empowerment, a new perspective, and transformation (♇) through his expansive (♃) career pursuits (Mc), which had a dramatic, major impact (♇) on countless people. Pasteurization, the process that bears his name, interestingly involves killing (♇) bacteria (also ♇). Through his research (♇ once again), Pasteur developed vaccines against anthrax and rabies by using dead or weakened bacteria (♇ references yet again) to induce formation of a beneficial (♃) antigen to protect the individual from a specific disease.

- Lucille Ball's AP = ♇ = ☉/♂ midpoint picture demonstrates the potential for public projection to have a major impact (♇) through focused, passionate, relentless energy and self-promotion (☉/♂).

- Actor Gregory Peck's AP = ♇ = ♀/♆ midpoint picture suggests a potential for public projection (AP) and a desire for empowerment, perspective, and transformation (♇) that can be accomplished through an idealistic approach and harmonious (♀) dreams or visions (♆). The idealism that pervaded his personal life reverberated in his role in *To Kill a Mockingbird*, which won him the Academy Award for Best Actor in 1962. Peck's poignant portrayal of Atticus Finch, a Depression-era attorney set on defending a black man accused of raping a local white girl, reflected his own idealistic need to make a dramatic difference (♇).

☊ contact with the AP—suggests the potential for public projection of an ability to easily connect with groups or with the public in general.

Both the North Node and the Aries Point have interpretive keywords associated with *the public*. Therefore, it is logical that whenever both the AP and the North Node are involved in a midpoint picture, the resultant influence represents a "double whammy" of potential for connectivity with the public at large.

- Baseball legend Pete Rose's North Node is at the Aries Point, which could bode well for his eventual induction into the hall of fame, but is challenged by the midpoint picture ☊ = ☿/♆. This picture suggests that the public (☊) may find some of his statements (☿) rather difficult to believe (♆).

- Buddy Holly has the same midpoint picture as Pete Rose, but it played out quite differently. AP = ☊ = ☿/♆ suggests that the potential for public projection could benefit through communicating (☿) imaginative dreams or visions (♆), or by creating a mental picture for the public through his music.

- Television psychologist Dr. Phil McGraw has AP = ☊ = ☽/♇, suggesting the potential for public projection (AP) with an amplified relationship with the public (☊) that can be accomplished through an intensity (♇) of emotions (☽) and a need to make a dramatic difference (♇) through use of these emotions (☽).

As mentioned previously, even if the North Node is not the Focal Point but instead represents one part of the right side of our midpoint picture equation, the influence is still noteworthy.

- Dustin Hoffman's closest AP-related midpoint picture is AP = ☊/Asc, suggesting that his potential for public projection could be accomplished by just being himself (Asc), and the public (☊) would embrace him. He has another midpoint picture involving the North Node, AP = ♃/☊, that further suggests that his relationship with the public (☊) would be on a relatively large, expansive (♃) scale.

- Even though we don't know Bob Hope's exact birth time, we can be assured that he has a midpoint picture that connects the Aries Point and the North Node with his AP = ♂ = ♃/☊. Unlike Dustin Hoffman's AP = ♃/☊, Mars is involved as an additional Focal Point in Bob Hope's midpoint picture. This suggests that his potential for public projection can be accomplished through focusing his energies (♂) on exposure to the public (☊) on a large scale (♃). Beyond his movies and television appearances, Hope's benevolent (♃) donation of time to the U.S.O. shows for the armed forces (♂) further elevated his already popular image with the public (☊).

Asc contact with the AP[29]—suggests the potential for public projection of an ability to easily align with public popularity, by having congenial personality traits conducive to public attraction.

- Television evangelist Jimmy Swaggart's AP = Asc = ♂/♄ = ♆/Mc suggests a potential for public projection through his personal image (AP = Asc) using fierce (♂) determination (♄), or perhaps through spiritual or deceptive (♆) means affecting his public image (Mc).

- Astrologer Noel Tyl's AP = Asc = ♃/☊ suggests his potential for public projection through use of his personality (Asc) in expansive (♃) dealings with the public (☊) and an effusive public persona. His career as an international (♃) opera singer, prior to his prolific astrological work, also allowed ample opportunities for public exposure.

- Karen Carpenter's midpoint picture AP = Asc = ☉/♆ suggests that her potential for public projection (AP) and identity definition (Asc) can be accomplished through illuminated (☉) imagination, dreams, or spirituality (♆). Unfortunately, her well-documented eating disorder may have at least partially stemmed from an unclear or distorted (♆) view of herself (both Asc and ☉).

Mc contact with the AP—suggests the potential for public projection to easily utilize the career or public image to attract public attention and exposure.

- John Nash's AP = Mc = ☿/♀ midpoint picture suggests the monumental task of trying to bring his thoughts and ideas (☿) into harmony (♀). Isn't it ironic that the biographical movie chronicling his life was called *A Beautiful* (♀) *Mind* (☿)? Another AP midpoint picture in his chart is Mc = ♄/♇, which symbolizes a rather public (Mc) struggle between an irresistible force (♇) and an immovable object (♄). This picture shows itself in Nash's life as a struggle (♄) with his psychological (♇) problems. It is also interesting to note that his AP = Mc = ♄/Asc suggests that he possesses the potential for eventually gaining control (♄) of himself (Asc).

- Ted Turner, owner of Turner Broadcasting, has the midpoint picture AP = Mc = ♀/♇, which suggests a potential for public projection (AP) and a public image (Mc) focused on aesthetic or social (♀) transformation and new perspectives (♇). This theme is validated both by Turner's donations to social causes and his commitment to the restoration (♇) of aesthetics (♀) through colorization and preservation of classic early films.

- Author Lewis Carroll's AP = Mc = ☽/♆ midpoint picture suggests career- (Mc) related potential for public projection (AP) that can be accomplished through pursuit of emotional needs (☽) related to idealism, imagination, dreams, or fantasy (♆). Carroll's *Alice in Wonderland* parallels his emotional (☽) sensitivity/vulnerability (♆) and gives the reader a glimpse into a fantastic—and often disorienting—journey. Perhaps Alice's experiences were intended to parallel and reflect one's introspection and the associated emotional (☽) ambiguities (♆) that are encountered on one's personal travels *Through the Looking Glass.*

Charts with No Focal Point in the Aries Point Region

As we have observed, not all charts have direct Focal Point contact with the Aries Point. It must be noted that even in charts with no AP contact with a Focal Point, there is still a relationship to midpoints that fall within the AP range. All charts without exception contain the AP locations, but these locations are not always occupied by either a Focal Point or a midpoint.

Using interpretive methods similar to those described in chapter 2 of this book, we can incorporate the Aries Point as a surrogate Focal Point to create a midpoint picture and a corresponding interpretation by using any midpoint within orb of the AP. The midpoint picture interpretation can then be modified slightly to add the "public thrust" dimension.

- Actor Tom Hanks has no Focal Point in the Aries Point area of the chart, but his AP = ☿/♀ delineates his potential for public projection through having a way with words. Hanks also has AP = ♄/♅, which aptly describes how he is able to project an extremely diverse range of roles because he can easily break (♅) with tradition (♄) and defy being typecast.

- Magician Roy Horn, of Siegfried and Roy, has AP = ☿/♆, suggesting that his potential for public projection can be accomplished through mental (☿) inspiration (♆) or by the communication (☿) of imaginative dreams or visions (♆). This midpoint picture could also describe the public projection (AP) of magic (♆) to deceive (♆) the senses (☿).

- In an interesting combination of analytical midpoint picture techniques, Bridget Bardot's AP = ☉/♀ suggests that her potential for public projection can be accomplished through an illumination (☉) of aesthetics (♀) or by being identified for her physical beauty. This is particularly appropriate to consider because both her Sun and Venus are unaspected natally.

- Even though we don't know the birth time of mathematician and logician René Descartes, it is certain that his Aries Point midpoint picture AP = ☿/♄ is valid because neither Mercury nor Saturn changes position appreciably in a single day. The potential for public projection (AP) can be accomplished through giving substance (♄) to thoughts, ideas, and communication (☿), or through creation of reality (♄) from thoughts (☿). It should come as no surprise that this Aries Point midpoint picture—

suggestive of what one will likely be remembered for—relates harmoniously to his most memorable quote, "I think, therefore I am."

- Existentialist philosopher Jean Paul Sartre has the midpoint ☉/♅ within orb of the AP, giving us the midpoint picture AP = ☉/♅. This picture suggests the potential for public projection (AP) that can be accomplished through an innovative, eccentric (♅) approach to life purpose (☉); an illumination (☉) of individuality (♅). "His philosophy of existentialism stated that the world had no meaning for mankind, but instead proposed that the individual is responsible for his or her own purpose."[30]

Special AP Midpoint Pictures

AP = ☉/☽—Whenever the AP is at the Sun/Moon midpoint, we often see a publicly displayed amplification of combined ego needs and emotional needs.

With the AP = ☉/☽, we often see a very public figure whose motivations and behaviors are consistent with what we would expect from the ☉-☽ Blend and personified, defined, and refined by the specific location of the ☉/☽ midpoint within the AP location. In many ways, the life becomes "an open book" in which the public has full access to intimate details of the individual's wants and needs.

It is helpful to incorporate the Sun and Moon signs to add depth to our analysis. Examples of famous people with their Sun and Moon signs are listed below.

- Timothy Leary's AP = Mc = ☉/☽ (☉ in ♎ and ☽ in ♒) and AP = Mc = ☉/♅ allowed (or compelled) him to do his own thing and to express his eccentricity very publicly.
- Jimi Hendrix (AP = ♆ = ☉/☽, with ☉ in ♐ and ☽ in ♋). Note that Neptune is associated with both "purple" and "haze," which is Hendrix's signature song "Purple Haze."
- Charles Kuralt of the *CBS Evening News'* "On the Road" segment has AP = ☿ = ☉/☽, with ☉ in ♍ and ☽ in ♎. This picture vividly describes the analytical (☉ in ♍) yet emotionally balanced (☽ in ♎) perspective Kuralt related on his travels (☿) around America.

For readers wishing to explore further, the following famous people have the AP at the Sun/Moon midpoint. The Sun and Moon signs are included for each.

- Rocker Mick Jagger of the Rolling Stones (AP = ♆ = ☉/☽, with ☉ in ♌ and ☽ in ♉)

- Astronomer and developer of the telescope Galileo Galilei (☉ in ♓ and ☽ in ♈)

- British Prime Minister Tony Blair (☉ in ♉ and ☽ in ♒)

- César Chavez (AP = ♅ = ☉/☽, with ☉ in ♈ and ☽ in ♓)

- Nat "King" Cole (☉ in ♓ and ☽ in ♎)

- Sir Arthur Conan Doyle (☉ in ♊ and ☽ in ♒)

- Hugh Hefner (AP = ☉/☽, with ☉ in ♈ and ☽ in ♓)

- Christine Jorgensen (AP = ♅ = ☉/☽, with ☉ in ♊ and ☽ in ♑)

AP = Asc/Mc—When the Aries Point is at the Mc/Asc midpoint, it suggests a consistency between the public (Mc) and private (Asc) personas, a commonality of the identity focus. One may identify so strongly with the career or the public image that the personal identity is absorbed or sacrificed. Aspects of the public and private life may become so intricately intertwined that the two may become virtually indistinguishable. This brings to the forefront in the public view both the public and the private aspects of one's life.

Famous people with AP = Asc/Mc include Muhammad Ali, Mae West, Christopher Reeve, Donald Trump, Tina Turner, Tony Blair, Charles Chaplin, F. Scott Fitzgerald, Greta Garbo, Sigmund Freud, and Martha Stewart.

The Closest Aries Point Midpoint Picture

As we would reasonably expect, it appears that the closer the Focal Point or midpoint is to the exact 0° Aries Point location, the more analytical weight it should be given as it applies to defining the potential for public projection.

Though all midpoint pictures within the defined range are interpretively helpful, *the midpoint picture closest to the AP* seems to carry with it a special weight, in that this closest midpoint picture so often graphically and accurately suggests how the potential for public projection can be demonstrated in the person's life. Adding the other AP-related midpoints can further refine the AP analysis.

If no Focal Point is within the AP range, then we simply find the midpoint that is nearest to 0° or 90° in the 90° Midpoint Sort.

As we examine Charles Dickens's 90° Midpoint Sort (figure 13), we see that there is no Focal Point within the Aries Point range. However, we find two midpoints in the AP range. We then calculate which of these midpoints is closest to the exact AP location (closest to either 0°00' or 90°00' on the 90° Midpoint Sort). For Charles Dickens, our calculations proceed this way:

AP = ♃/♄ at 0°26'

0°26'
minus 0°00'
0°26' away from the exact 0°00' AP location

AP = ♂/Asc at 88°11'

90°00' (remember that there are *sixty minutes* [60'] in each degree)
minus 88°11'
1°49' away from the exact 90°00' AP location

Therefore, Charles Dickens's closest Aries Point midpoint picture is AP = ♃/♄, suggesting a potential for public projection (AP) through overcoming (♃) obstacles and limitations (♄) and through highlighting extreme ups (♃) and downs (♄). The opening sentence of his epic *A Tale of Two Cities*, in which he relates to his vast readership the extreme polarities of existence, eerily echoes this midpoint picture: "These were the best of times (♃), these were the worst of times (♄)."

Charles Dickens *Feb 07, 1812* *07:50:00 PM LMT* *001W05'00" 50N48'00"*

Midpoint Sort: 90° Dial

♃/♄	000°26'	☿	022°10'	♃/☊	032°51'	☿/♇	049°36'	☉/♂	072°45'	♃/♆	079°45'
☽/☿	002°23'	☉/♃	022°14'	☉/☿	035°04'	☿/Asc	050°30'	☽/♆	072°49'	♃/Mc	081°01'
☿/♆	002°35'	☽/☊	025°54'	♀/♃	036°23'	♂/♄	050°58'	♆	073°01'	☿/♅	082°43'
☿/Mc	003°51'	♆/☊	026°06'	♃/♇	036°46'	♅	053°15'	♇/☊	073°07'	♂/☊	083°22'
♄	004°22'	☉/♄	026°10'	♄/☊	036°47'	☉/☊	058°35'	♄/♅	073°49'	☽/♄	083°29'
☉/♅	005°36'	☊/Mc	027°22'	♃/Asc	037°40'	☿/♂	059°51'	☊/Asc	074°01'	♄/♆	083°42'
♂	007°33'	☽/♀	029°26'	☽/♂	040°05'	☉/♀	062°07'	☽/Mc	074°04'	♄/Mc	084°57'
☿/♃	009°20'	♀/♆	029°38'	♂/♆	040°17'	☉/♇	062°30'	♆/Mc	074°16'	♃	086°29'
☿/♄	013°16'	☽/♇	029°50'	♀/♄	040°19'	☽/♅	062°56'	Mc	075°32'	♀/♂	086°54'
☽/☉	015°17'	♆/♇	030°02'	♄/♇	040°42'	♅/♆	063°08'	♀	076°16'	♂/♇	087°18'
☉/♆	015°29'	♂/♅	030°24'	♂/Mc	041°32'	☉/Asc	063°24'	♀/♇	076°39'	♂/Asc	088°11'
♅/☊	016°13'	☽/Asc	030°43'	♄/Asc	041°36'	♅/Mc	064°24'	♇	077°03'		
☉/Mc	016°45'	♀/Mc	030°54'	☿/☊	045°41'	☊	069°12'	♀/Asc	077°33'		
♀/♅	019°45'	♆/Asc	030°55'	♂/♃	047°01'	♃/♅	069°52'	♇/Asc	077°56'		
♅/♇	020°09'	♇/Mc	031°17'	☉	047°58'	☽	072°36'	Asc	078°50'		
♅/Asc	021°02'	Mc/Asc	032°11'	☿/♀	049°13'	♀/☊	072°44'	☽/♃	079°33'		

Figure 13. Charles Dickens's 90° Midpoint Sort

Following are other famous people with their closest Aries Point midpoint pictures.

- Jim Jones, the Guyana cult leader who led his followers to mass suicide, has as his closest Aries Point midpoint picture AP = ♆/Mc. His potential for public projection (AP) was through a spiritual, inspirational, or even deceptive (♆) public image (Mc). Poison, coincidentally, also has a Neptunian association.

- Miss Cleo, the purported psychic who gained notoriety for her psychic hot line "infomercials" on television, has AP = ☉/♆ as her closest Aries Point midpoint picture. This midpoint picture suggests that the potential for public projection (AP) can be accomplished through illuminated (☉) imagination (♆), identity (☉) ambiguities (♆), or perhaps a distorted portrayal (♆) of self (☉). The TV ads claimed that she was born in Jamaica, although numerous consumer complaints related to questionable company practices revealed that she was really born in Los Angeles. The enterprise eventually was sued for fraud of various sorts and forced to cease operations.

- Hugh Hefner, with his AP = ☿/♅ (within 0°01' orb), suggesting potential for public projection (AP) through innovative, nontraditional, unconventional, and perhaps radical (♅) communication (☿), certainly supports the development and publication of *Playboy* magazine and allowed Hefner to get his message out unreservedly (i.e., relatively free of censorship).

- Adolf Hitler's AP = ♂/♄ translates as the potential for public projection (AP) that can be accomplished through a fierce determination (♂) to conquer obstacles (♄). Fittingly, his autobiographical treatise was called *Mein Kampf (My Struggle)*. A second midpoint in Hitler's chart ties for the closest to the Aries Point. It is AP = ♀/♄, making aesthetic beauty (♀) tangible (♄), which fits in with Hitler's demented concept of a perfect race that could be developed only by strict (♄) social (♀) controls (♄).

- The Marquis de Sade has AP = ♇/Mc, suggesting the potential for public projection (AP) through shaking things up publicly (Mc) or needing to change the world in a dramatic fashion (♇). In this case, Pluto took a decidedly sexually explicit (♇) turn.

- Actor-Governor Arnold Schwarzenegger has AP = ♃/♄ as his closest AP midpoint picture, suggesting that his potential for public projection (AP) can be accomplished through an optimistic (♃) view of reality (♄) or by pushing (♃) the limits (♄).

- Liberace, the flamboyant performer, has AP = ☽/Asc as his closest AP midpoint picture, suggesting that his potential for public projection (AP) can be accomplished through nurturing emotional needs (☽) by defining the identity (Asc).

If, however, there is a Focal Point in the AP region of the 90° Midpoint Sort, then we are faced with a decision. We need to decide between two options:

1. We can use the midpoint that is nearest to 0° or 90° in the 90° Midpoint Sort, as previously described.
2. Alternatively, we can use the midpoint falling within the AP range that is *closest to the Focal Point.*

Admittedly, this is a fine point, but one that bears explanation. In my research, I used the second method. My rationale is that any Focal Point found within the AP range is deserving of maximum importance in the overall analysis of the potential for public projection. While all the AP midpoint pictures are important, the main focus should lie primarily with the Focal Point, and secondarily with the associated midpoints.

George Lucas *May 14, 1944 05:40:00 AM PWT 121W00'00" 37N39'00"*

Midpoint Sort: 90° Dial

☉/♇	000°04'	☽/♄	018°20'	♅/♆	034°50'	☽/♃	044°54'	♆/♇	064°07'	☽/☿	084°04'
♀/♃	000°09'	☿/♆	019°16'	☽/Mc	035°09'	☉/☿	045°12'	♄/Asc	066°18'	☊/Asc	084°09'
♆	001°41'	♀/♆	021°44'	☽/☊	036°11'	Asc	047°13'	☽/♆	066°29'	♀/♇	084°10'
♂/♅	001°42'	♃/♄	021°57'	♇	036°33'	☉/♀	047°41'	♅	068°00'	☉/♂	084°29'
☽/☉	002°26'	♆/Asc	024°27'	☿	036°50'	♃	048°31'	☉/♄	069°28'	♄	085°22'
♃/Asc	002°52'	♂	025°23'	♂/♃	036°57'	☉/Asc	050°24'	♃/♆	070°06'	☉/Mc	086°17'
♅/Mc	003°30'	♂/Mc	027°11'	♃/Mc	038°45'	☿/♅	052°25'	☿/♂	076°07'	☽/♀	086°33'
♅/☊	004°32'	☉/♆	027°38'	☽/♇	038°55'	☉	053°34'	♄/♅	076°41'	♇/Asc	086°53'
☉/♃	006°02'	♂/☊	028°14'	☿/♀	039°19'	♀/♅	054°54'	☿/Mc	077°55'	☉/☊	087°19'
♅/♇	007°16'	Mc	028°59'	♃/☊	039°47'	♅/Asc	057°37'	♀/♂	078°36'	☿/♃	087°41'
☽/♅	009°39'	☊/Mc	030°02'	☽	041°18'	♂/♆	058°32'	☿/☊	078°57'	☽/Asc	089°16'
♂/♄	010°23'	♂/♇	030°58'	♀	041°48'	♆/Mc	060°20'	♀/Mc	080°24'		
♄/Mc	012°11'	☊	031°04'	☿/Asc	042°02'	☉/♅	060°47'	♂/Asc	081°18'		
♄/☊	013°13'	♇/Mc	032°46'	♃/♇	042°32'	☿/♄	061°06'	♀/☊	081°26'		
♃/♅	013°15'	☽/♂	033°21'	♄/♆	043°32'	♆/☊	061°22'	☿/♇	081°42'		
♄/♇	015°58'	♇/☊	033°48'	♀/Asc	044°30'	♀/♄	063°35'	Mc/Asc	083°06'		

Figure 14. George Lucas's 90° Midpoint Sort

In figure 14, we see the 90° Midpoint Sort for George Lucas. Neptune qualifies as a Focal Point within the Aries Point range, but we want to find the closest midpoint picture.

To choose the closest Aries Point midpoint picture using the options just described, we can choose between the two alternatives:

1. AP = ♆ = ☉/♇, because the Sun/Pluto midpoint is the *closest to the Aries Point*, being just 0°04' away from exact.

2. AP = ♆ = ♂/♅, because the Mars/Uranus midpoint is the *closest to the Focal Point* Neptune.

While either choice will give a meaningful midpoint picture interpretation, as I said, I choose the second option because it connects the Focal Point with its nearest midpoint to create our closest Aries Point midpoint picture.

Using the first option, George Lucas's Neptune is involved in the Aries Point midpoint picture AP = ♆ = ☉/♇. Interpretively, this midpoint picture suggests a creatively visualized and inspired (♆) potential for public projection (AP) that can be accomplished through a display of powerful (♇) ego (☉) urges or a compelling need to leave one's mark and to provide a groundbreaking influence.

Using the second option, George Lucas's Neptune figures prominently in his Aries Point midpoint picture AP = ♆ = ♂/♅, suggesting an energetic, relentless drive (♂) toward individualistic expression (♅), possibly even risk taking. This certainly portends well for the connection to the public through his imaginative movies (♆), especially the futuristic *Star* (♅) *Wars* (♂) series.

Under normal circumstances, I would look at both of these midpoint pictures but give an amplified interpretive value to the second option.

In the following example, because Neptune is also unaspected, it deserves even greater attention in the analysis of midpoint pictures.

- Television evangelist Jimmy Swaggart has AP = Asc = ♆/Mc as his closest Aries Point midpoint picture. This midpoint picture suggests that the potential for public projection and identity definition (Asc) can be accomplished through a spiritual or inspirational (♆) career or public image (Mc). This was certainly the case, as he built a tremendously loyal and lucrative following. However, the darker side of this midpoint picture emerged when some well-publicized (AP) personal (Asc) indiscretions were uncovered. Behind-the-scenes (♆) behavior developed into a public (AP and Mc) embarrassment, leading to a dramatically televised personal (Asc), tearful (♆), public (Mc) confession (♆).

Most of us have learned from experience that any specific astrological technique may be difficult to interpret when applied solely by itself. But when we combine it with other influences suggested in the context of the complete horoscope, we begin to see a more detailed, rather homogeneous—and simultaneously complicated—portrait develop. So, rather than examining just a single isolated part, the chart as a whole must be considered.

The AP is no exception to this rule. For example, the astrologer should routinely consider the sign, house, rulership, and aspects relating to the AP to seek clarification in the overall interpretation. This process of incorporating AP contact into chart synthesis allows a distinctly embellished dimension of the horoscope to emerge.

It is fascinating to see the wide range of possible manifestations associated with the specific Focal Point's keywords. For example, when Neptune is in contact with the AP, one finds examples of tremendously diverse extremes ranging from inspired, selfless spirituality to outright fraud or deception. Interestingly, sometimes *both extremes* are exhibited in the life of a single individual.

As with all midpoint pictures, Aries Point midpoint pictures often reflect or reinforce the themes that may have already been suggested and considered in the preliminary analysis of the natal chart. At times, though, these midpoint pictures may reveal a totally different, otherwise unidentified, or unnoticed point of emphasis within the personality.

Whenever the anticipated Aries Point potential is *not* demonstrably projected publicly in the individual's life, we need to find out *why*. It may have been delayed or derailed due to challenges within the developmental process, or the individual may not be fully aware of how this potential for public projection can be accessed and pursued.

As a personal example, I have AP = Asc = ♅/Mc in my horoscope. This suggests a potential for public projection in an unusual or unconventional manner to define the identity, or the pursuit of an unusual, out-of-the-mainstream career. Relatively late in my life, I found that these influences could no longer be ignored. After twenty-six years in an established, accepted profession in the medical field, I made a radical career switch at age fifty to the much less traditional line of work as an astrologer.

---

1. Lois Rodden's AstroDatabank biographical information (www.astrodatabank.com). Parenthetical astrological associations added by author.
2. Ibid.

3. Although we don't know Mickey Mouse's "birth" time, the Walt Disney Company recognizes Mickey's birth date as November 18, 1928.

4. AstroDatabank biographical information. Parenthetical astrological associations added by author.

5. *The American Heritage Dictionary of the English Language*, 4th ed., s.v. "Capraesque."

6. AstroDatabank biographical information. Parenthetical astrological associations added by author.

7. Ibid.

8. AstroDatabank biographical information. Parenthetical astrological associations added by author.

9. The context of Churchill's exact quotation may have been lost. For a discussion of this quotation's origin, please refer to http://www.wsu.edu/~brians/errors/nonerrors.html.

10. Noel Tyl, *Synthesis & Counseling in Astrology* (St. Paul, MN: Llewellyn Publications, 1994).

11. Please note the subtle differences in notation between the Sun-Moon Blend (☉-☽ with a *dash* separating the luminaries) and the Sun/Moon midpoint (☉/☽ separated by a *forward slash*).

12. AstroDatabank biographical information. Parenthetical astrological associations added by author.

13. Major aspects for the purposes of this book are the Ptolemaic aspects: the conjunction, square, opposition, trine, and sextile.

14. House rulerships establish a relationship between a particular planet and the house(s) with the associated sign on its cusp (e.g., if Leo is on the tenth-house cusp, then the Sun is said to rule the tenth house, or alternatively, the tenth house is ruled by the Sun), and that planet has an implied connection to the matters of the involved house(s).

15. Mutual receptions form a connection between two planets, each of which is in the other's ruling sign (e.g., when the Sun is in Capricorn and Saturn is in Leo).

16. The personal planets include the Sun, Moon, Mercury, Venus, and Mars. The condition of these planets by sign, house, house rulership, etc., typically relates intimately to the behavior of the individual.

17. The quintile (glyph = Q) is a 72° minor aspect suggesting creativity.

18. *The Quotations Page*, http://quotationspage.com/quotes/Errol_Flynn.

19. *ThinkExist.com*, http://en.thinkexist.com/quotation/a_man_should_not_strive_to_eliminate_his/145649.html.

20. *ThinkExist.com*, http://en.thinkexist.com/quotation/what_progress_we_are_making-in_the_middle_ages/219116.html.

21. AstroDatabank biographical information. Parenthetical astrological associations added by author.

22. *ThinkExist.com*, http://en.thinkexist.com/quotation/my_hope_still_is_to_leave_the_world_a_bit_better/344369.html.

23. *ThinkExist.com*, http://en.thinkexist.com/quotation/great_ambition_is_the_passion_of_a_great/294512.html.

24. *ThinkExist.com*, http://en.thinkexist.com/quotation/i_have_always_known_what_i_wanted-and_that_was/211807.html.

25. Note that the 2° orb from a Focal Point will often extend beyond the Aries Point region of the chart. In such cases, it is safe to assume that while the effect of such midpoints beyond the Aries Point range will still have an Aries Point–type potential to connect with the Focal Point, these midpoints would be expected to have a lesser effect than midpoints located within the Aries Point range.

26. As mentioned previously, while the midpoint ♃/Asc is within orb of the Sun, it is itself beyond the range of the Aries Point; therefore, it would have less effect than those midpoint pictures with the midpoint located within the Aries Point range.

27. AstroDatabank biographical information.

28. Please also see AP = Mc/Asc in the "Special AP Midpoint Pictures" section in this chapter.

29. Interestingly, it is not uncommon to see a natal square between the Asc and Mc. When this condition exists and either point is at the AP, we will often see both the Asc and the Mc within orb of the AP.

30. AstroDatabank biographical information.

CHAPTER FOUR

Integration and Synthesis

Making mental connections is our most crucial learning tool,
the essence of human intelligence; to forge links;
to go beyond the given; to see patterns, relationships, context.

—MARILYN FERGUSON, AUTHOR

Midpoint Analysis Example

In the following example, we will bring together everything we have learned about midpoint analysis. We will identify, interpret, and integrate all we learn about this individual as we assess the midpoint pictures.

For this example, we will use the Midpoint Worksheet (figure 15). The worksheet is shown with entries reflecting the midpoint pictures for the current example. This worksheet is provided only as a guideline. You may choose to modify it to meet your own needs and preferences. In general, the more important measurements are identified in the top section of the template, with secondary—but still important—midpoint pictures identified in the bottom section. The top section includes what I consider to be the crucial categories of midpoint analysis. Even if we were to curtail our analysis after completing the top section, we would have gained a wealth of information through the midpoint picture interpretation. A blank copy of the Midpoint Worksheet is included in appendix V.

As you fill in the worksheet, if a midpoint picture has already been identified in a previous category, you may choose to slightly modify the previous impression to include the suggestion from the current category.

We begin our analysis with the 90° Midpoint Sort in figure 16 and the 90° Midpoint Tree in figure 17.

AP = __/__ (88°00'–2°00' on 90° Midpoint Sort)	Potential for public projection; what we will potentially be remembered for	AP = ☽ = ♄/♅ = ☊/Asc = ♃/♆ = ♆/♇ = ☿/♄ = ☉/☊
Unaspected Planet(s)[1] (UP) 1) UP as Focal Point 2) Two UP in midpoint 3) One UP in midpoint	Gives analytical insight into UP interpretation; helps to integrate UP	1) ☉ = ♆/Mc = ♂/♃ = ♄/♇ = ♂/♇ ♀ = ☿/♇ = ♂/♆ = ♅/♇ = ♄/♆ ♂ = ♆/☊ = ☽/Asc = ♀/♃ 2) ☿ = ☉/♀ (☿ linked to two UP) ☊ = ☉/♂ (☊ linked to two UP) 3) not used in this example[2]
Focal Point = ☉/☽ (☉ & ☽ signs may be used)	Connects ego and emotional needs; forms the core of relationship dynamics	♂ = ☉/☽ (2°05' orb) (☉ ♑ and ☽ ♎)
Focal Point = Asc/Mc	Identity awareness; links personal and public focus; merging of internal and external	— (But ☉/☽ = Asc/Mc)
Closest midpoint picture	Often identifies a dominant theme in the individual horoscope	♆ = ☿/♅
Combinations of these planets in the midpoint:[3] →	**Suggest:**	
☽, ☿, ♀, or ♆	Idealism; aesthetics; creativity	♃ = ☽/☿ ♄ = ☽/☿ ♅ = ☽/☿ ☊ = ☿/♆ Asc = ☽/♆
☉, ♂, ♄, or ♇	Power or control needs	☉ = ♂/♇*[4] ☉ = ♄/♇* ☊ = ☉/♂* Asc = ♄/♇*
☿, ♂, ♃, or ♅	Impatience, restlessness, impulsiveness, recklessness	☉ = ♂/♃* ♆ = ☿/♅* Mc = ☿/♂
☿ & ♄	Putting thoughts or ideas into a tangible form	☽ = ☿/♄*
♂ & ♆	Charisma; inspiration to act	♀ = ♂/♆*
♃ & ♄	Expansion vs. restraint; overcoming restrictions	Asc = ♃/♄
♄ & ♅	Old vs. new; control vs. freedom	☽ = ♄/♅*

Figure 15. Midpoint Worksheet Example

Template Analysis

Midpoint Sort: 90° Dial

☽	000°00'	~~☽/♆~~	~~015°06'~~	♆	030°11'	~~♃/♅~~	~~046°03'~~	~~☽/♅~~	~~060°34'~~	~~♂/Asc~~	~~079°10'~~
♄/♅	000°06'	~~♃/♄~~	~~015°07'~~	~~♅~~	~~031°02'~~	~~⊖/Mc~~	~~048°26'~~	~~♃~~	~~061°03'~~	~~⊖/♄~~	~~080°50'~~
☊/Asc	000°28'	~~⊖/☿~~	~~020°54'~~	~~☊/Mc~~	~~035°09'~~	~~Mc/Asc~~	~~049°41'~~	~~♀/Mc~~	~~063°45'~~	~~♀/♆~~	~~081°40'~~
♃/♆	000°37'	~~⊖/♅~~	~~021°46'~~	~~⊖/♇~~	~~035°25'~~	~~♀/♇~~	~~050°44'~~	~~♂/☊~~	~~064°38'~~	~~♄/Asc~~	~~082°05'~~
~~♀/♂~~	~~003°14'~~	~~♇/☊~~	~~022°00'~~	~~☿/♀~~	~~036°13'~~	☽/☉	051°15'	~~⊖/♆~~	~~066°21'~~	~~Mc~~	~~084°22'~~
~~♀/♄~~	~~006°10'~~	~~☿/Asc~~	~~022°08'~~	~~♇/Asc~~	~~036°40'~~	♀/♃	052°06'	~~☽/♀~~	~~066°34'~~	~~☿/♂~~	~~086°19'~~
~~☿/☊~~	~~007°37'~~	~~♅/Asc~~	~~023°01'~~	~~⊖/♃~~	~~036°47'~~	☽/Asc	052°30'	~~♄/☊~~	~~067°33'~~	~~☽/Mc~~	~~087°11'~~
~~♅/☊~~	~~008°29'~~	~~♃/☊~~	~~023°30'~~	~~♀/♅~~	~~037°05'~~	♆/☊	053°04'	~~♆/Asc~~	~~067°35'~~	~~♂/♅~~	~~087°11'~~
♂/♇	010°50'	~~♂/Mc~~	~~023°51'~~	~~☽/☊~~	~~037°58'~~	♂	053°20'	~~♇/Mc~~	~~071°21'~~	☉/☊	089°13'
♂/♃	012°11'	~~☽/♂~~	~~026°40'~~	~~♃/Asc~~	~~038°01'~~	~~♂/♄~~	~~056°15'~~	~~♃/Mc~~	~~072°43'~~	☿/♄	089°14'
♆/Mc	012°17'	~~♄/Mc~~	~~026°46'~~	♂/♆	041°46'	~~☿/Mc~~	~~056°50'~~	~~☽/♇~~	~~074°10'~~	♆/♇	089°16'
☉	012°30'	☉/♀	027°49'	♀	043°09'	~~♅/Mc~~	~~057°42'~~	~~☿/♆~~	~~074°44'~~		
♄/♇	013°45'	~~♀/Asc~~	~~029°04'~~	☿/♇	043°49'	~~♇~~	~~058°20'~~	~~☽/♃~~	~~075°32'~~		
~~⊖/Asc~~	~~013°45'~~	☿	029°17'	♄/♆	044°41'	~~♄~~	~~059°10'~~	~~♅/♆~~	~~075°37'~~		
~~♀/☊~~	~~014°32'~~	~~☽/♄~~	~~029°35'~~	♅/♇	044°41'	☽/☿	059°39'	☊	075°56'		
~~Asc~~	~~014°59'~~	☿/♅	030°10'	~~☿/♃~~	~~045°10'~~	~~♃/♇~~	~~059°42'~~	☉/♂	077°55'		

Figure 16. Midpoint Analysis Example 90° Midpoint Sort

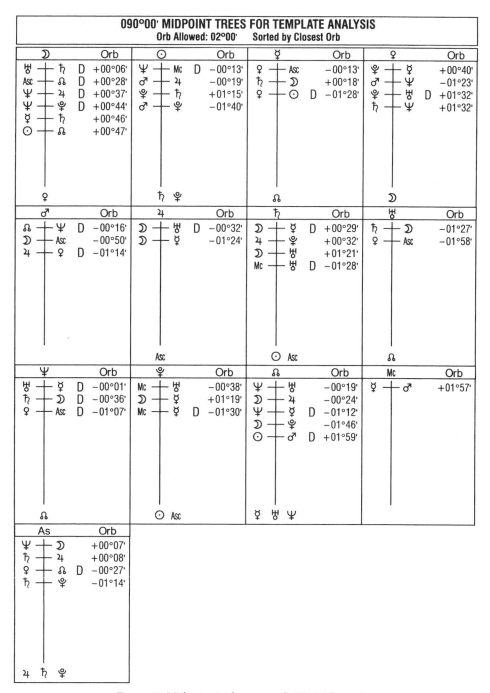

Figure 17. Midpoint Analysis Example 90° Midpoint Tree

Aries Point

With the Moon being located exactly at the Aries Point (0°00' on the 90° Midpoint Sort), we find that there are six individual midpoint pictures within a 2° orb when using both the AP and the Moon as co-Focal Points. Using our sentence construction technique of interpretation, we could begin the analysis of each of these six midpoint pictures reflecting the combined impact of the Aries Point with the natal Moon by saying:

> *The potential for public projection (AP) by connecting emotionally (☽) with the public in order to nurture, protect, or provoke an emotional response (☽) can be accomplished through...*

AP = ☽ = ♄/♅
: *breaking (♅) rules (♄), breaking (♅) with tradition (♄), or gaining stability (♄) by using an innovative (♅) approach.*

AP = ☽ = ☊/Asc
: *establishing an intimate (Asc) connection with the public (☊).*

AP = ☽ = ♃/♆
: *an expansive, optimistic, inspirational, or unrestricted (♃) imaginative dream or vision (♆); possibly excessive (♃) escapism (♆) or opinionation (♃).*

AP = ☽ = ♆/♇
: *imagination or a vision (♆) that can yield a dramatic outcome (♇).*

AP = ☽ = ☿/♄
: *giving substance or structure (♄) to thoughts or ideas (☿); creation of reality (♄) from thoughts, ideas, or communication (☿); possible oppressive or depressive (♄) thoughts (☿).*

AP = ☽ = ☉/☊
: *thriving on public attention (☊), personal popularity (☉), and public exposure (☊).*

To summarize these AP midpoint pictures in a couple of sentences, we could say:

> *The potential for public projection by connecting emotionally with the public can be accomplished through an intimate yet nontraditional way of communicating. Public appeal, personal popularity, and the ability to communicate and give meaning to expansive thoughts and visions can inspire a dramatic emotional impact.*

Unaspected Planets

Not all charts have unaspected planets. However, in this example we identify *three* unaspected planets from the aspect grid in figure 18. There are no major (Ptolemaic) aspects that connect the Sun, Venus, or Mars with any other planet.[5] It is relatively uncommon to find this many unaspected planets in any given chart, so we welcome any information that can help us to better understand the suggested motivations and potentials associated with each of these unaspected planets.

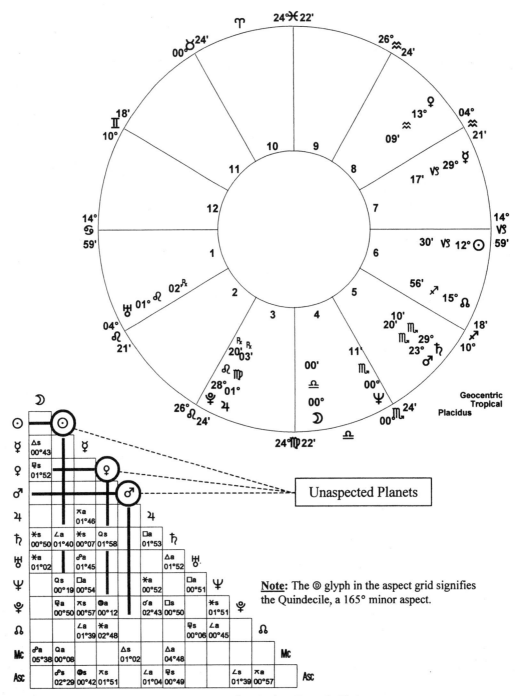

Note: The ⊚ glyph in the aspect grid signifies the Quindecile, a 165° minor aspect.

Figure 18. Template Analysis Example Chart

When the all-important **Sun is unaspected**, there is usually no lack of energy, but a pronounced need to find a focus for this energy. *The life purpose and ego definition (☉) can be accomplished through...*

☉ = ♆/Mc   *use of a spiritual or inspirational (♆) public image (Mc); possible unclear (♆) public image (Mc), concealed (♆) public behavior (Mc), or public (Mc) deception (♆).*

☉ = ♂/♃   *energetic (♂) optimism, expansion, and confidence (♃) or by working (♂) for a cause (♃); possible opinionated (♃) energy (♂).*

☉ = ♄/♇   *increased stability (♄) through major changes or sacrifice (♇); a power (♇) struggle (♄) between the status quo (♄) and necessary, inevitable change (♇).*

☉ = ♂/♇   *promoting (♂) a new perspective (♇); lighting the fuse of intense (♇) passion (♂); provoking (♂) a major change (♇); possible intimidation (♇) or violent actions (♂).*

Summarizing the **unaspected Sun** midpoint pictures:

Life purpose and ego definition can be accomplished through an energetic use of a spiritual or inspirational public image to promote and bring about dramatic, meaningful change.

With **unaspected Venus**, *social, aesthetic, or relationship needs can be accomplished through...*

♀ = ☿/♇   *communication (☿) of profound, deep concepts (♇).*

♀ = ♂/♆   *use of charisma (♂/♆) and energetically (♂) sharing a vision (♆) or inspiring (♆) action (♂); possible unclear or veiled (♆) motives (♂).*

♀ = ♅/♇   *sudden, possibly disruptive or radical (♅) activity for growth, rebirth, or dramatic change (♇); possible disruptive (♅) upheaval (♇).*

♀ = ♄/♆   *giving substance (♄) to the dream (♆); making the intangible (♆) tangible (♄); clarifying (♄) the nebulous (♆); possible clouded (♆) sense of reality (♄), blurred or unclear (♆) boundaries (♄).*

Summarizing the midpoint pictures for **unaspected Venus**:

> *Social, aesthetic, or relationship needs can be accomplished through a willingness to take radical action to charismatically communicate the vision or by a conviction that by taking dramatic action, the dream can become a reality.*

With **unaspected Mars**, *efficient use of energy can be accomplished through...*

$\sigma = \Psi / \Omega$ *a vision (Ψ) being shared with the public (Ω); a chameleonlike (Ψ) public image (Ω); possible deception or concealing something (Ψ) from the public (Ω).*

$\sigma = \mathcal{D} / \text{Asc}$ *nurturing emotional ($\mathcal{D}$) needs through setting an example (Asc); emotional ($\mathcal{D}$) introspection (Asc).*

$\sigma = \Omega / \mathfrak{4}$ *embracing harmony, justice, and social (Ω) convictions ($\mathfrak{4}$); possible overindulgence or excess ($\Omega / \mathfrak{4}$).*

Summarizing the midpoint pictures for **unaspected Mars**:

> *Efficient use of energy can be accomplished through a publicly shared, personally demonstrated vision of harmony, fairness, and social justice.*

In addition to the midpoint pictures in which the Focal Point represents an unaspected planet, we have two midpoint pictures that contain *two of the three unaspected planets* in the midpoint (i.e., on the right side of the midpoint equation).

- The first such midpoint picture, $\Psi = \odot / \Omega$, illustrates a connection between the Focal Point Mercury and both the unaspected Sun and unaspected Venus. This midpoint picture suggests that:

  > *Efficient thoughts and communication (Ψ) can be accomplished through an illumination ($\odot$) of aesthetics (Ω) or by seeing ($\odot$) the beauty (Ω).*

- The second midpoint picture links the unaspected Sun and unaspected Mars while utilizing the North Node as the Focal Point, giving us $\Omega = \odot / \sigma$. This midpoint picture suggests:

Relationships and connection with the public (☊) can be accomplished through utilization of energy (♂) in a determined, assertive pursuit (♂) of life purpose and identity definition (☉); a passionate, relentless energy (♂); self-promotion (☉/♂).

The Sun/Moon Midpoint

There is no Focal Point within a 2° orb of the Sun/Moon midpoint, but if the parameters are stretched just a bit, we find ♂ = ☉/☽ within an orb of 2°05', comfortably within our extended 2°30' maximum range of orbs for midpoints involving the ☉/☽.

The importance of the Sun/Moon midpoint is such that we are almost obligated to include any midpoint picture that is so close to falling within the 2° orb. Again, orbs represent personal preferences, so it is important to trust your own impulses and experiences. If you feel strongly that the orb should be extended in some cases by another half degree (i.e., up to 2°30'), then by all means do so. Remember that with orbs, there is no right or wrong. Just ask yourself, "Is it *reasonable* to include this particular measurement even though it stretches my usual limits a little?" There is no harm in including a borderline measurement now and then. Chances are that if you feel compelled to even consider the inclusion of a particular measurement, you probably should go ahead and use it. Now that you have endured yet another of my obligatory orb oratories, let me attempt to get back on track.

As we interpret the ♂ = ☉/☽ midpoint picture, we come up with:

Efficient use of energy (♂) can be accomplished through the pursuit and integration of ego needs (☉) and emotional needs (☽).

If we want to expand the meaning of the Sun/Moon midpoint even further, we can incorporate the respective signs of the Sun and Moon. In this case, the Sun in Capricorn and the Moon in Libra allow us to embellish the interpretation:

Efficient use of energy (♂) can be accomplished through the pursuit and integration of ego needs (☉) for sustained progress through disciplined ambition (☉ in ♑) while pursuing the need to please and be appreciated (☽ in ♎) through embracing emotional harmony and fairness.

The Ascendant/Midheaven Midpoint

With the Ascendant/Midheaven midpoint located at 49°41' on the 90° Midpoint Sort, we find no Focal Point within 2° (or even within our maximum orb of 2°30') of this midpoint, so there is no Focal Point associated with the Asc/Mc midpoint in this example.

However, the Asc/Mc midpoint is within orb of the ☉/☽ midpoint. As discussed in chapter 3, the proximity of these two important midpoints to one another suggests a unity of focus with substantial common ground connecting the ego, emotional needs, and the expression of identity—both on a personal level and through the public image or the career.

Closest Midpoint Picture

The closest midpoint picture, ♆ = ☿/♅, is just 0°01' of orb away from being exact.

> *Enlightenment, inspiration, or escape needs* (♆) *can be accomplished through innovative, unconventional, or even radical* (♅) *thoughts, ideas, and communication* (☿); *by speaking* (☿) *unreservedly* (♅).

Other Midpoint Pictures

I intentionally chose this rather complicated example because it involves many more midpoint pictures than are typically encountered using the Midpoint Worksheet due to the number of Aries Point midpoint pictures and the three unaspected planets.

There are additional midpoint pictures that fall within a 2° orb. As you perform your first midpoint analyses, I suggest that you interpret all the applicable midpoint pictures for at least a few charts. Ideally, this is good to do with your own chart or that of a significant other—someone that you know really well. The subtleties of the midpoint pictures are almost like subtitles in a foreign film—they allow us to understand what is going on with the players on a deeper level.

Continuing with our example, the bottom part of the Midpoint Worksheet in figure 15 contains several categories that identify significant midpoint pictures. Using the combination of planets in the midpoint,[6] the bottom section of the worksheet describes previously unidentified midpoint pictures in several categories. (Note that midpoint pictures that previously have been identified are indicated with an asterisk on the example worksheet.)

Idealism, Aesthetics, and Creativity

Three midpoint pictures are identified that contain the ☽/☿ midpoint. Incorporating three different Focal Points, we arrive with these midpoint pictures and the combined interpretations:

♃ = ☽/☿ ⎫
♄ = ☽/☿ ⎬ *Optimism and expansion (♃), necessary controls (♄), and the desire for*
♇ = ☽/☿ ⎭ *sweeping, dramatic change (♇) can be accomplished through emotional (☽) communication (☿).*

We also find in this category:

☊ = ☿/♆ *A relationship with the public (☊) can be accomplished through communication (☿) of imaginative dreams or visions (♆); possible confused, distorted, or deceptive (♆) thoughts or communication (☿).*

Asc = ☽/♆ *Identity definition and personal projection (Asc) can be accomplished through nurturing emotional needs (☽) by imagination, dreams, or fantasy (♆); possible emotional (☽) confusion or deception (♆).*

Power or Control Needs

Asc = ♄/♇ *Identity definition and personal projection (Asc) can be accomplished through a power struggle between the status quo (♄) and necessary, inevitable change (♇); increased stability (♄) as a result of major change or sacrifice (♇).*

Impatience, Restlessness, Impulsiveness, Recklessness

Mc = ☿/♂ *Career pursuits or public image (Mc) can be accomplished through energetic, assertive (♂) thoughts and communication (☿), or through provocative or controversial (♂) ideas or communication (☿).*

Expansion versus Restraint or Overcoming Restrictions

Asc = ♃/♄ *Identity definition and personal projection (Asc) can be accomplished through cautious (♄) optimism (♃) or by overcoming (♃) limitations (♄); or by pushing (♃) the limits (♄).*

After you get into the rhythm of doing midpoint analysis, you probably won't feel compelled to look in depth at *all* the midpoint pictures for each chart you do. That was my assumption when I developed the Midpoint Worksheet template. Having the template available to act as a reminder of the most important midpoint pictures minimizes the chance of missing a major one. Obviously you may choose to include more or fewer midpoint pictures.

Okay, So Who Is It?

I know many of you may have been wondering about the identity of the mystery example. Perhaps it has been a bit cruel to make you wait (wade?) through all this analysis to find out that this astrological data belongs to the actor Mel Gibson.[7] Now that you know who it is, you probably will want to revisit this section and examine the suggestions that we derived from the of his midpoint pictures. Doing so will reaffirm the premise that we can understand general developmental themes—sometimes with substantial detail—while hardly referring to the natal chart. As we learn more about an individual during the interactive consultation, we can use midpoint pictures to further fine-tune our analysis.

The following midpoint pictures reflect Mel Gibson's extraordinary popularity and also identify some potential problem areas:

AP = ☽ = ☊/Asc

AP = ☽ = ☉/☊

These two midpoint pictures combined suggest his potential for public projection to easily relate emotionally on a personal level with the public, but also emphasize that his actions are exposed to public view, for better or worse.

In July 2006, after being stopped for speeding, Gibson's arrest on suspicion of DUI resulted in his well-publicized, emotionally charged verbal outburst.[8] Gibson later issued a statement that confirmed his lifelong struggle with alcoholism and offered an apology for his "horrific relapse."

Astrologically, we see multiple cautionary statements interspersed throughout Gibson's midpoint picture analysis. Many of these measurements demonstrate the full range of expression—both positive and challenging—that he has experienced.

Multiple Neptune references are associated with films or movies but can also refer to escapism, confusion, or disorientation. Jupiter references highlight a powerful strength of conviction and a possible tendency to overdo or overindulge.

Gibson's high-profile life, as suggested by the multiple Aries Point references, assures that the coverage of his past and future behavior will continue to be subjected to intense public scrutiny. Other specific midpoint pictures describing the range of expression that has been demonstrated in Gibson's professional and private life are briefly discussed below.

The ♂ = ☉/☽ midpoint picture suggests that his energetic drive, his disciplined ambition to make progress (☉ in ♑), and his emotional need for harmony and to be appreciated (☽ in ♎) represent the central focus in his life. This need to please and be appreciated (as suggested by the Moon in Libra) combines with the attractive, charismatic image (♀ = ♂/♆) appropriate for winning acclaim as "the sexiest man alive." The ♂/♆ midpoint also cautions against possible confusing (♆) actions or behavior (♂).

His bad-boy, independent, eccentric, free-spirited image is exemplified in the midpoint picture AP = ☽ = ♄/♅. This describes not only his real-life rule-breaking behavior, but also the traits of the character in his breakthrough performance as a likeable (☽) but slightly off-kilter (♅) cop (♄) in *Lethal Weapon*. This midpoint picture also provides the emotional link (☽) between the past (♄) and the future (♅) for the masses in the *Mad Max* films, as his character brought structure and stability (♄) to some violently chaotic (♅) situations.

In retrospect, it is interesting to note that another of Gibson's midpoint pictures—this one with his unaspected Sun as the Focal Point, ☉ = ♂/♇—could be interpreted as:

Ego definition (☉) *can be accomplished through a role in* Lethal (♇) Weapon (♂).

While there is no possible way that we realistically could have predicted the exact name of the movie that was to become (at that point in his career) his defining role, it is still quite mind-boggling to see how appropriate these natal midpoint pictures often prove to be. Gibson's roles in *Lethal Weapon* and the *Mad Max* films established and defined him as the consummate courageous hero (♂ and ☉) who is willing to use violence (♂ and ♇) when necessary. Cautionary suggestions associated with this midpoint picture include intense passion and possible intimidation or violent actions.

The hero role—well described by Gibson's ♂ = ♀/♃ midpoint picture—proves to be central to his character portrayal in some of his most memorable films. Often there is also a strong focus on using his energy (♂) with social (♀) conviction (♃) for what is right, as in the movie *Braveheart*, which chronicled the life of Scottish hero William Wallace. This same midpoint picture also shows his personal activity (♂) in real life for social (♀) causes (♃) and his reputation as a generous philanthropist (♃).

Unaspected Sun and Mars are connected to the North Node in the midpoint picture ☊ = ☉/♂. This picture symbolizes the connection with the public, and is particularly appropriate for the public acclaim (☊) he received related to his Academy Awards for Best Picture and Best Director for *Brave* (♂) *heart* (☉).

The midpoint picture ☉ = ♂/♃ describes ego definition achievable through working for a cause, and fits in well with his role in *The Patriot* as well as his other heroic roles. The "Damn the torpedoes, full speed ahead!" attitude exemplified by this midpoint picture demonstrates the unlimited (♃) confidence (♂) in himself (☉) that was shown in his energetic (♂) personal (☉) support and funding (♃) of *The Passion of the Christ*, a huge financial (♃) and personal (☉) success (♃) despite the odds. In Gibson's personal life, this midpoint picture comes into play through a personal expression (☉) of opinionated (♃) energy (♂).

Gibson's willingness—perhaps even emotional need (☽)—to break (♅) the rules (♄) is exemplified in the Aries Point midpoint picture AP = ☽ = ♄/♅. Despite the risk or danger (♅) suggested here, his risks generally have led to greater stability (♄). The independent, rebellious nature (♅) suggests strongly that he is—and has been—content (compelled?) to break away from (♅) the traditional, the expected, or the status quo (♄), both in his acting roles and in his professional life.

Some of the most powerful suggestions derived from Mel Gibson's midpoint pictures involve his ability to project publicly (AP) on an emotional level (☽) by being able to communicate his thoughts and ideas (☿) in a tangible form (♄), as demonstrated astrologically by the Aries Point midpoint picture AP = ☽ = ☿/♄.

His public affability (♀) allows him to communicate (☿) profound, deep concepts (♇), as shown by the ♀ = ☿/♇ midpoint picture. Meanwhile, his energy (♂) is used to share a vision (♆) with the public (☊), as demonstrated by the ♂ = ♆/☊ midpoint picture, and benefits from his chameleonlike (♆) public image (☊) by acting in various roles. Caution is advised, however, for Gibson to avoid an unclear or confusing (♆) public (☊) impression.

We gain a better understanding of Mel Gibson as an actor, a director, and a person particularly after seeing how his career and personal life have played out the potential suggested by the midpoint pictures in his astrological chart.

Midpoint Analysis with an Unknown Birth Time

Working with unknown birth times is a challenge that astrologers frequently encounter. The process of *rectification*[9] can often yield considerable insight into the birth time, but can prove to be a lengthy and sometimes tedious process.

One alternative to a full rectification that I've found to be quite useful is the incorporation of midpoints into the analysis of a natal chart when the exact birth time cannot be determined definitively.

Midpoint pictures can either reinforce suggestions from the natal chart or can suggest areas that are not obvious from the natal chart. These subtle but powerful indicators can be quite useful even when we don't know the birth time; however, we must determine which midpoint pictures to use and which ones to exclude.

When analyzing midpoint pictures for charts with an undetermined birth time, we must necessarily exclude from consideration any planet or point whose position changes appreciably in a given twenty-four-hour period. We can immediately eliminate the Ascendant and Midheaven from consideration, as they pass through the entire zodiac every single day. Secondly, we must also exclude the rapidly moving Moon from consideration. Mercury, the next fastest-moving planet, doesn't move significantly in a twenty-four-hour period, so we will opt to include it in the midpoint analysis. Assuming that we must eliminate the Ascendant, Midheaven, and Moon from consideration, the number of potential midpoints decreases dramatically.

It is possible to do a midpoint analysis for a chart with an unknown or uncertain birth time by using either the 90° Midpoint Sort or the 90° Midpoint Tree. For this example, I will illustrate both forms. With any midpoint analysis, I prefer to use both forms, as I've found this combination presents the easiest and most direct approach. To review the differences between the two forms, please refer to appendix I.

When using the 90° Midpoint Sort *without the Midpoint Tree* (see figure 19A) we must do the following:

1. Identify any midpoints in the Aries Point areas (enclosed in solid boxes in the illustration).

2. Exclude any midpoints that include the Moon, Ascendant, or Midheaven, as well as the individual listings for these points (shown with a solid line through them).

Unknown Birthtime

Midpoint Sort: 90° Dial											
☿/☊	001°23'	♆	016°20'	♄/♆	029°37'	~~☽/♃~~	~~044°50'~~	~~☉/Asc~~	~~062°16'~~	☉/♄	080°03'
♄/♇	001°46'	☿/♂	016°29'	♃/♅	030°36'	~~☽/☉~~	~~046°16'~~	~~☽~~	~~065°19'~~	♂	080°38'
~~Mc~~	~~003°44'~~	☉/♀	016°29'	☉/♅	032°02'	☿/♇	046°29'	♃/♆	065°20'	~~☽/Asc~~	~~081°19'~~
~~♀/Mc~~	~~004°45'~~	~~♅/Mc~~	~~020°10'~~	☿/♃	033°20'	♄/☊	046°40'	♂/☊	065°32'	♃/☊	082°23'
♇/☊	005°32'	♂/♇	020°38'	♆/☊	033°23'	♂/♆	048°29'	☉/♆	066°46'	☉/☊	083°49'
♀	005°45'	♀/♅	021°19'	~~☽/Mc~~	~~034°32'~~	☊	050°26'	~~♅/Asc~~	~~067°05'~~	♄/♅	084°53'
~~Asc~~	~~007°19'~~	~~☿/Mc~~	~~023°02'~~	☉/☿	034°46'	~~Mc/Asc~~	~~050°32'~~	~~♄/Mc~~	~~068°19'~~	~~☽/♆~~	~~085°50'~~
♂/♃	007°29'	☿/♀	024°03'	~~☽/♀~~	~~035°32'~~	♇	050°39'	♀/♄	069°20'	~~♂/Mc~~	~~087°11'~~
☉/♂	008°55'	♃	024°20'	♅	036°52'	~~☽/♅~~	~~051°06'~~	~~☿/Asc~~	~~069°49'~~	☿/♄	087°37'
~~☽/♄~~	~~009°07'~~	~~♄/Asc~~	~~025°07'~~	♃/♇	037°30'	~~♀/Asc~~	~~051°32'~~	♅/♆	071°36'	♀/♂	088°12'
~~♆/Asc~~	~~011°50'~~	☉/♃	025°46'	☉/♇	038°55'	~~☽/☿~~	~~053°49'~~	~~☊/Mc~~	~~072°05'~~	♅/☊	088°39'
~~☽/☊~~	~~012°53'~~	~~♇/Mc~~	~~027°11'~~	☿/♅	039°36'	~~♆/Mc~~	~~055°02'~~	♀/☊	073°06'		
♂/♅	013°45'	☉	027°12'	☿	042°20'	♀/♆	056°03'	~~♇/Asc~~	~~073°59'~~		
~~♃/Mc~~	~~014°02'~~	~~☽/♂~~	~~027°50'~~	♄	042°54'	~~☽/♇~~	~~057°59'~~	☿/♆	074°20'		
♀/♃	015°03'	♀/♇	028°12'	♅/♇	043°45'	~~♃/Asc~~	~~060°50'~~	♆/♇	078°29'		
~~☉/Mc~~	~~015°20'~~	~~☊/Asc~~	~~028°53'~~	~~♂/Asc~~	~~043°59'~~	♂/♄	061°46'	♃/♄	078°37'		

Figure 19A. Filtered 90° Midpoint Sort for Unknown Birth Time (Moon, Ascendant, and Midheaven Excluded)

3. Next, we exclude any midpoints that are not within orb of the remaining Focal Points. (These midpoints also have a solid line through them in figure 19B.)

Unknown Birthtime

Midpoint Sort: 90° Dial											
☿/☊	001°23'	♆	016°20'	~~♄/♆~~	~~029°37'~~	~~☽/♃~~	~~044°50'~~	~~☉/Asc~~	~~062°16'~~	☉/♄	080°03'
♄/♇	001°46'	☿/♂	016°29'	~~♃/♅~~	~~030°36'~~	~~☽/☉~~	~~046°16'~~	~~☽~~	~~065°19'~~	♂	080°38'
~~Mc~~	~~003°44'~~	☉/♀	016°29'	~~☉/♅~~	~~032°02'~~	~~☿/♇~~	~~046°29'~~	~~♃/♆~~	~~065°20'~~	~~☽/Asc~~	~~081°19'~~
~~♀/Mc~~	~~004°45'~~	~~♅/Mc~~	~~020°18'~~	~~☿/♃~~	~~033°20'~~	~~♄/☊~~	~~046°40'~~	~~♂/☊~~	~~065°32'~~	♃/☊	082°23'
♇/☊	005°32'	~~♂/♇~~	~~020°38'~~	~~♆/☊~~	~~033°23'~~	♂/♆	048°29'	~~☉/♆~~	~~066°46'~~	~~☉/☊~~	~~083°49'~~
♀	005°45'	~~♀/♅~~	~~021°19'~~	~~☽/Mc~~	~~034°32'~~	☊	050°26'	~~♅/Asc~~	~~067°05'~~	~~♄/♅~~	~~084°53'~~
~~Asc~~	~~007°19'~~	~~☿/Mc~~	~~023°02'~~	~~☉/☿~~	~~034°46'~~	~~Mc/Asc~~	~~050°32'~~	~~♄/Mc~~	~~068°19'~~	~~☽/♆~~	~~085°50'~~
♂/♃	007°29'	☿/♀	024°03'	~~☽/♀~~	~~035°32'~~	♇	050°39'	~~♀/♄~~	~~069°20'~~	~~♂/Mc~~	~~087°11'~~
~~☉/♂~~	~~008°55'~~	♃	024°20'	♅	036°52'	~~☽/♅~~	~~051°06'~~	~~☿/Asc~~	~~069°49'~~	~~☿/♄~~	~~087°37'~~
~~☽/♄~~	~~009°07'~~	~~♄/Asc~~	~~025°07'~~	♃/♇	037°30'	~~♀/Asc~~	~~051°32'~~	~~♅/♆~~	~~071°36'~~	♀/♂	088°12'
~~♆/Asc~~	~~011°50'~~	~~☉/♃~~	~~025°46'~~	~~☉/♇~~	~~038°55'~~	~~☽/☿~~	~~053°49'~~	~~☊/Mc~~	~~072°05'~~	♅/☊	088°39'
~~☽/☊~~	~~012°53'~~	~~♇/Mc~~	~~027°11'~~	~~☿/♅~~	~~039°36'~~	~~♆/Mc~~	~~055°02'~~	~~♀/☊~~	~~073°06'~~		
~~♂/♅~~	~~013°45'~~	☉	027°12'	☿	042°20'	~~♀/♆~~	~~056°03'~~	~~♇/Asc~~	~~073°59'~~		
~~♃/Mc~~	~~014°02'~~	~~☽/♂~~	~~027°50'~~	♄	042°54'	~~☽/♇~~	~~057°59'~~	~~☿/♆~~	~~074°20'~~		
♀/♃	015°03'	♀/♇	028°12'	♅/♇	043°45'	~~♃/Asc~~	~~060°50'~~	~~♆/♇~~	~~078°29'~~		
~~☉/Mc~~	~~015°20'~~	~~☊/Asc~~	~~028°53'~~	~~♂/Asc~~	~~043°59'~~	~~♂/♄~~	~~061°46'~~	~~♃/♄~~	~~078°37'~~		

Figure 19B. Filtered 90° Midpoint Sort for Unknown Birth Time (Moon, Ascendant, and Midheaven Excluded)

4. Finally, we need to identify the midpoint pictures from the remaining Focal Points and midpoints within a 2° orb.

Alternatively, if we choose to use both the 90° Midpoint Sort and the 90° Midpoint Tree, the operation becomes substantially more straightforward. We then need only identify any midpoints in the Aries Point areas from the 90° Midpoint Sort (as in figure 19), excluding any entries that contain the Moon, Ascendant, or Midheaven as the Focal Point or as a component of the midpoint. We then can proceed to the 90° Midpoint Tree to continue the process.

Using the 90° Midpoint Tree (figure 20), we can go through and strike out any listing that contains the Moon, Ascendant, or Midheaven. This is less cumbersome than using the 90° Midpoint Sort exclusively, as all midpoints that are beyond the 2° orb already are excluded.

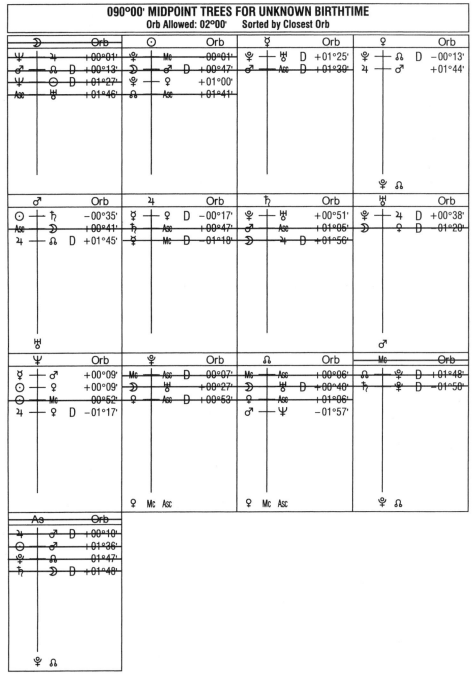

Figure 20. 90° Midpoint Tree for Unknown Birth Time

Some astrology software programs, such as Win*Star by Matrix Software, allow us to define which planets or points are included in the 90° Midpoint Tree. By using this option to exclude the Moon, Ascendant, and Midheaven, the same midpoint pictures are identified more easily. The resultant midpoint tree includes only those midpoints within orb and displays only what is needed for this midpoint analysis.

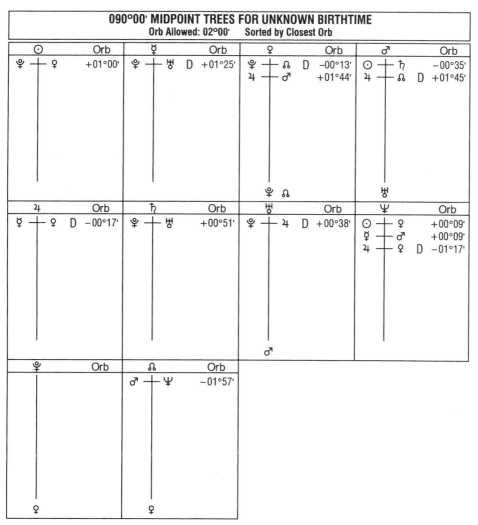

*Figure 21. Filtered 90° Midpoint Tree for Unknown Birth Time Example
(Moon, Ascendant, and Midheaven Excluded)*

We now only need add in the Aries Point midpoint pictures from the 90° Midpoint Sort to begin the analysis. For this example, we will use the Midpoint Worksheet for Unknown Birth Times (figure 22). This worksheet is provided only as a guideline. You may choose to modify it to meet your own needs and preferences. The worksheet template is shown with entries reflecting the midpoint pictures for the current example. A blank form is included in appendix VI for your convenience.

As you fill in the worksheet, if a midpoint picture already has been identified in a previous category, you may choose to slightly modify the previous impression to include the suggestion from the current category.

AP = __/__ (88°00'–2°00' on 90° Midpoint Sort)	Potential for public projection; what we will potentially be remembered for	AP = ☿/☊ = ♄/♇ = ♀/♂ = ♅/☊
Focal Point = ☉	Helps to define identity and personal projection in absence of a known Asc	☉ = ♀/♇
Unaspected Planet(s)[10] (UP) 1) UP as Focal Point 2) Two UP in midpoint 3) One UP in midpoint	Gives analytical insight into UP interpretation; helps to integrate UP	♅ is the only UP 1) ♅ = ♃/♇ 2) — 3) ☿ = ♅/♇, ♄ = ♅/♇
Closest midpoint picture	Often identifies a dominant theme in the individual horoscope	♇ = ☉/♀ ♇ = ☿/♂
Combinations of these planets in the midpoint:[11]	→ **Suggest:**	
☿, ♀, or ♇	Idealism; aesthetics; creativity	♃ = ☿/♀
☉, ♂, ♄, or ♇	Power or control needs	—
☿, ♂, ♃, or ♅	Impatience, restlessness, impulsiveness, recklessness	♀ = ♂/♃
☿ & ♄	Putting thoughts or ideas into a tangible form	—
♂ & ♇	Charisma; inspiration to act	☊ = ♂/♇
♃ & ♄	Expansion vs. restraint; overcoming restrictions	—
♄ & ♅	Old vs. new; control vs. freedom	—

Note: In cases of unknown birth times, we must exclude any pictures that include the Asc, Mc, or ☽. The positions of the other planets and the North Node do not change enough in a 24-hour period to appreciably affect midpoint pictures.

Figure 22. Midpoint Worksheet for Unknown Birth Times Example

Aries Point

For each of these Aries Point midpoint pictures, we can prefix the interpretation with: *There is a potential for public projection through...*

AP = ☿/☊   *easily sharing thoughts, ideas, and communication (☿) with the public (☊).*

AP = ♄/♇   *increased stability (♄) as a result of major change or sacrifice (♇); tremendous efforts (♄) for dramatic changes (♇); the symbolic meeting of an irresistible force (♇) with an immovable object (♄); a monumental power (♇) struggle (♄) between the status quo (♄) and necessary, inevitable change (♇).*

AP = ♀/♂   *use of energy (♂) for an aesthetic or social (♀) purpose; awareness of the male- (♂) female (♀) energies; sexual energy; intimate relationships.*

AP = ♅/☊   *an innovative (♅) relationship with the public (☊); unconventional or revolutionary (♅) approaches to public (☊) issues; taking public (☊) risks (♅).*

The Sun as the Focal Point

If the birth time is unknown, we must sacrifice any insight regarding the identity or personal projection that could be suggested by the Ascendant position. To partially compensate for not knowing the Ascendant, any midpoint pictures with the Sun as the Focal Point become particularly important, as they give us insight into the core urges of the individual, which would otherwise remain unknown. In this example, we find a single midpoint picture with the Sun at the Focal Point:

☉ = ♀/♇   *Life purpose and ego definition (☉) can be accomplished through aesthetic or social (♀) transformation (♇); a new perspective (♇); or dramatic social (♀) change (♇).*

Unaspected Planet(s), Part 1

Also, with an unknown birth time, we cannot be sure if there are any unaspected planets, because the position of the Moon is unknown. Again, based on the known information, I assign an added emphasis to planets that are unaspected with another planet, and, in this case, exclude the Moon as well. In this example, we find that Uranus is the only unaspected planet. There is a single midpoint picture with Uranus at the Focal Point.

♅ = ♃/♇   *Individualistic expression or innovation (♅) can be accomplished through a strength of conviction and optimism (♃) for dramatic sweeping change (♇); expansive (♃) transformational change (♇) or growth (♃); recognizing, embracing, or promoting necessary inevitable change (♇); potential for major recognition or financial rewards (♃).*

Unaspected Planet(s), Part 2

There is only one unaspected planet, so we proceed to part 3.

Unaspected Planet(s), Part 3

To gain further insight into the unaspected planet, we consider any midpoint picture in which Uranus is part of the midpoint (i.e., on the right side of the equation). We find two midpoint pictures with different Focal Points sharing the same midpoint (♅/♇). We can easily combine both Focal Points (☿ and ♄) into a single phrase:

☿ = ♅/♇
and
♄ = ♅/♇

Efficient thoughts, ideas, and communication (☿) as well as structure, stability, and necessary controls (♄) can be accomplished through sudden (♅), dramatic, possibly destructive change for growth or rebirth (♇); big changes (♇) for innovation (♅); radical (♅) restructuring of perspective (♇); disruptive (♅) upheaval (♇).

The Closest Midpoint Picture

With an unknown birth time, we cannot be certain of the closest midpoint picture. Even so, I have found it instructive to include the closest midpoint picture that remains after excluding the Moon, Ascendant, and Midheaven. In our example, there is a two-way tie for the closest midpoint picture.

♆ = ☉/♀   *Inspiration, creative visualization, or escape needs (♆) can be accomplished through an illumination (☉) of aesthetics or social issues (♀); by seeing (☉) the beauty (♀); by feelings of contentment.*

♆ = ☿/♂   *Inspiration, creative visualization, or escape needs (♆) can be accomplished through energetic, assertive, or forceful (♂) thoughts, ideas, or communication (☿); inciting action (♂) through words (☿); provocative, motivational, or argumentative (♂) communication (☿); controversial (♂) thoughts, ideas, or communication (☿).*

These two interpretations could be combined to suggest that:

> *Inspiration, creative visualization, or escape needs can be accomplished through*
> *energetically and forcefully advancing thoughts and ideas, or inciting aesthetic or*
> *social action through words.*

Bottom Section of the Worksheet for Unknown Birth Times

As we continue with our analysis on the bottom section of the Midpoint Worksheet, several previously unidentified midpoint pictures are identified in these categories:

Idealism, Aesthetics, or Creativity

♃ = ☿/♀   *Optimism, expansion, rewards, and recognition (or excesses) (♃) can be accomplished through beautiful, harmonious, balanced (♀) thoughts, ideas, and communication (☿); having a way with words (☿).*

Impatience, Restlessness, Impulsiveness, or Recklessness

♀ = ♂/♃   *Social, aesthetic, or relationship needs (♀) can be accomplished through energetic (♂) optimism, expansion, growth, confidence, and success (♃); flamboyant, feeling unstoppable, invincible; demanding (♂) respect (♃); working (♂) for a cause (♃); opinionated (♃) energy (♂); over-the-top self-promotion; "Damn the torpedoes, full speed ahead!"*

Charisma and Inspiration to Act

☊ = ♂/♆   *The relationship with the public (☊) can be accomplished through charisma (♂/♆); an energetic (♂) sharing of the dream or vision (♆); inspiring (♆) to action (♂); or unclear or veiled (♆) motives (♂).*

Other Midpoint Pictures

After we have completed the Midpoint Worksheet for Unknown Birth Times, we could reasonably end our analysis. However, the remaining midpoint pictures are included to provide a complete listing of all midpoint pictures. In practice, you can use as few or as many midpoint pictures as you feel comfortable with.

♀ = ♇/☊   *Social, aesthetic, or relationship (♀) needs can be accomplished through involvement in major, dramatic (♇), public (☊) changes.*

♂ = ☉/♄   *Efficient utilization of energy (♂) can be accomplished through a determined, ambitious, structured (♄) approach to life purpose and ego definition (☉); or a controlled, restrained (♄) ego (☉).*

♂ = ♃/☊   *Efficient utilization of energy (♂) can be accomplished through optimistic, expansive (♃) dealings with the public (☊); through an effusive (♃) public (☊) persona.*

♆ = ♀/♃   *Inspiration, creative visualization, or escape needs (♆) can be accomplished through expansive (♃) beauty (♀); harmony (♀), justice, and fairness (♃); social (♀) conviction (♃); overindulgence or excess; too much (♃) of a good thing (♀).*

As we compile all of our midpoint observations into a general summary, it is appropriate to take note of and to assign additional reliability to suggestions that are mentioned more than once or that exhibit some measure of overlap in their interpretations. For example, based on the multiple Uranus references, it is reasonable to anticipate that this individual is likely to be innovative, eccentric, or something of a nonconformist, perhaps even an outright rebel. Likewise, we take note of the repeated references to aesthetic or social themes as symbolized by Venus. There are also several references to Pluto, suggesting the Plutonian themes of empowerment, perspective, and transformation—as well as power needs, perhaps necessary destruction for rebirth. Multiple references to the North Node combine with the four powerful Aries Point midpoint pictures to suggest a significant relationship with the public.

Without any further suspense, I'll tell you whose chart information we have just analyzed. It is the multifaceted Benjamin Franklin.[12] Franklin was charismatic, curious, innovative, and inventive. He was also a risk taker and a skillful communicator, perhaps best known for his kite-flying experiment during the lightning storm, his role as an early statesman, and his service as one of the framers of the Declaration of Independence.

It is interesting to note that all of the observations in this example are made without knowing the sign or house position of any of the planets or being aware of any specific aspects between the planets. It is amazing to see the depth of interpretation that is possible from midpoint picture analysis *without having seen the natal chart* and—as in this example—*without a birth time*. Yet we still are able to anticipate significant details of the individual's potential from just this limited information.

Obviously, we usually would use the midpoint analysis as an adjunct to the natal chart analysis, allowing an even greater depth of scrutiny.

It is to our advantage to utilize applicable midpoint pictures even when we are uncertain of the birth time. The resultant insight from midpoint analysis is readily available and can help us to clarify and enhance the depth of the consultation when a complete rectification is not an option.

---

1. Unaspected planets make no major (Ptolemaic) aspects to another planet, and are abbreviated in this template as "UP."

2. If multiple UP midpoint pictures are identified in parts 1 and 2 of this section, then we can skip to part 3.

3. Appearing on the right-hand side of the midpoint picture equation.

4. An asterisk follows midpoint pictures that previously have been identified on this worksheet.

5. As we determine the unaspected status of a planet, remember that we consider only the Ptolemaic aspects (the conjunction, square, opposition, trine, and sextile) and exclude from consideration all minor aspects and all aspects to the North Node, Ascendant, or Midheaven.

6. Appearing on the right-hand side of the midpoint picture equation.

7. Mel Gibson's birth data from AstroDatabank is January 3, 1956, at 4:45 p.m. EST in Peekskill, NY (Rodden Rating = B).

8. For astrological insight into this event, please refer to the "Closest Midpoint Picture" section on page 142.

9. Rectification is the process of formulating a birth time when definitive records are unknown or unavailable.

10. Unaspected planets (UP) make no major (Ptolemaic) aspects to another planet.

11. Appearing on the right-hand side of the midpoint picture equation.

12. AstroDatabank lists Ben Franklin's birth data as January 17, 1706, at 10:30 a.m. LMT in Boston, MA (Rodden Rating = DD, indicating that there are multiple or conflicting birth times recorded).

CHAPTER FIVE

Advanced Midpoint Techniques

What we call chaos is just patterns we haven't recognized.

—CHUCK PALAHNIUK

Transits, Progressions, and Solar Arcs to Midpoints

The interpretive use of midpoints and midpoint pictures can be expanded beyond natal analysis. Contact with a Focal Point—by transit, progression, or solar arc—highlights time periods when the interpretive dynamic of the associated midpoint picture is particularly pronounced.

For example, when a transiting planet contacts a natal Focal Point, the transiting planet imparts its energies to both the Focal Point *and* any natal midpoint pictures connected to that Focal Point. Fortunately, this isn't nearly as complicated as it sounds.

In figure 23, the inner chart shows Jim Henson's natal chart while the outer chart shows the transits for November 11, 1969. We see that transiting Jupiter is approximately conjunct Henson's natal Venus. So in addition to the traditional interpretation of this transit, Jupiter also affects any natal midpoint picture that has Venus as the Focal Point.

The interpretation of this specific transit on the associated midpoint pictures could be prefaced with a phrase utilizing keywords for both Jupiter and Venus: *There is a **current focus** (the transit) on expansion, rewards, and recognition (♃) relating to social, aesthetic, or relationship (♀) needs that can be accomplished through . . .*

♀ = ♇/Asc *self-empowerment, a new individual (Asc) perspective (♇), and a powerful, dramatic personal projection.*

♀ = ♂/♃ *energetic (♂) and optimistic confidence and growth (♃).*

In another example from figure 23, the transiting North Node is conjunct Henson's natal Saturn. It follows that the North Node will influence not only Henson's natal Saturn but also any midpoint pictures having Saturn at the Focal Point. Interpretively, we could preface any such midpoint pictures with: *There is a **current focus** (the transit) on the relationship with the public (☊) relating to the construction of a strong and stable foundation (♄) through . . .*

♄ = ♅/♇ *innovative (♅) and dramatic changes (♇).*

♄ = ♂/Mc *an energetic (♂) pursuit of career (Mc) and public self-promotion.*

These examples highlight a tremendously important time in Jim Henson's life. On November 11, 1969, Henson and the Muppets began their long-term relationship with PBS Television on *Sesame Street*.

Obviously, when we look at transits, we aren't limited to just conjunctions. The conjunctions were used in this example merely to simplify the illustration. The exact nature of an influence will depend on the particular planets and the aspect involved. While a detailed discussion of transits, progressions, or solar arcs would require much more space than is available here, it is important to be aware how these applications relate to midpoint pictures. Readers are encouraged to use the references cited in the bibliography for further exploration.

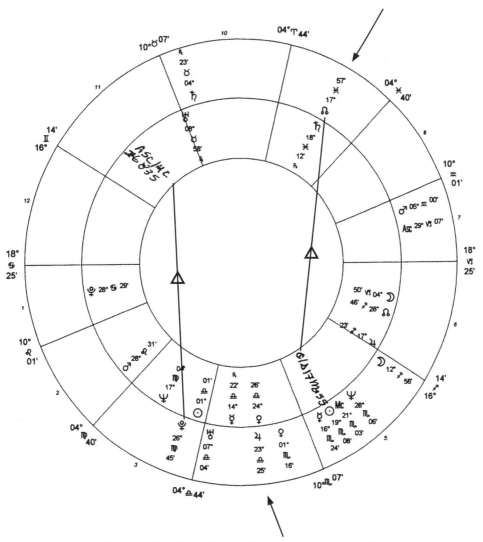

Figure 23. Jim Henson, Transit Chart for November 11, 1969

Jim Henson, Natal Chart (Inner Ring)
September 24, 1936 / Greenville, MS / 12:10 AM CST
Placidus Houses

Jim Henson, Transits for November 11, 1969 (Outer Ring)
November 11, 1969 / Alexandria, VA / 12:00 PM EST
Placidus Houses

More about Transits, Progressions, or Solar Arcs to Midpoints

As discussed in the previous example, transits, progressions, or solar arcs to the Focal Point of midpoint pictures can be used to gain insight into the specific influences at any particular time. We can also examine transits, etc., to specific midpoints that are *not within orb of any Focal Point*. While this method could be used to examine contact made by a transit, etc., to any midpoint, it is of particular importance when the "big two" midpoints—the Sun/Moon midpoint and the Ascendant/Midheaven midpoint—are involved.

Jim Henson's natal Sun/Moon midpoint is located at 17°55' Scorpio. At the time of the *Sesame Street* transits, we see the North Node at 17°57' Pisces, a 0°02' orb away from an exact trine to Henson's natal ☉/☽ midpoint. The trine to the ☉/☽ midpoint suggests a current (the transit) window of opportunity (△) for a relationship with the public (☊) and a harmonious relationship to support Henson's ego needs (☉ in ♎), and also fills his emotional need to make things happen (☽ in ♑).

The same principle can be applied to transits to the Asc/Mc midpoint of any natal chart, where the influence exerted by the transiting planet and its aspect affects both the personal identity and the public image. Referring once again to figure 23, we see transiting Pluto at 26°45' Virgo almost exactly trine Henson's Asc/Mc midpoint at 26°35' Taurus. This measurement suggests a current focus on (the transit) and a window of opportunity (△) for dramatic change, with empowerment, a new perspective, and transformation affecting both the personal identity and the public image (Asc/Mc midpoint).

Special Aspect Structures and Their Midpoint Pictures

As this segment correlating special aspect structures and midpoints began to germinate, one thing led to another, sometimes quite unexpectedly. Perhaps it was a frenetic fascination that began as I was looking again at some of M. C. Escher's intriguing graphic art. The way that he fit seemingly unrelated patterns together so seamlessly was mesmerizing. Coexisting themes thrived together with not a whit of wasted space—everything was where it needed to be; everything was where it *belonged.*

The parallels between Escher's art and astrology gradually became more evident, then almost *obvious.* The natal chart represents similar perfection, all represented on that single sheet of paper! Between its borders is a wealth of possibilities, probabilities, and potential that is so complete, so concise, and so compelling to try to comprehend.

As is the case with Escher's intricate patterns, the horoscope contains much more information than we can hope to fathom at first glance. We can only try to understand it layer by layer, observing how the individual bits and pieces fit together so perfectly and, in the process, add depth to our perceptions.

Special aspect structures[1] in the horoscope capture our attention with their intricate geometric patterns. Their symmetrical configurations beckon us to explore their interpretive symbolism. The following pages describe several specific aspect structures. Some of these structures are commonly referred to, while others are not. Each example begins with a description of the special aspect structure and then identifies the associated midpoint pictures that are implied and described within the structure.

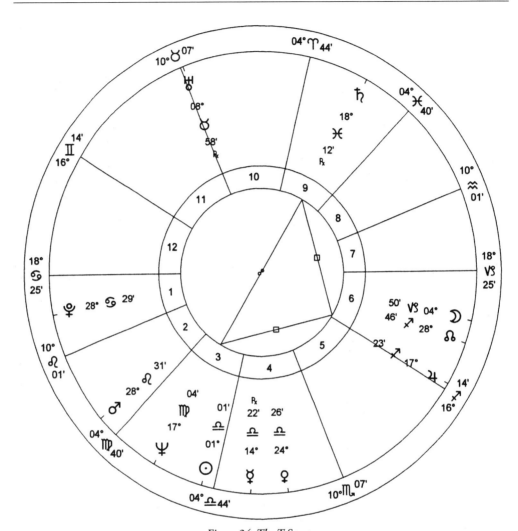

Figure 24. The T-Square

Jim Henson
September 24, 1936 / Greenville, MS / 12:10 AM CST
Placidus Houses

The T-Square

We have mentioned previously the T-Square formation, in which two natal planets or points in opposition to one another are both squared by a single planet or point. In the 90° format, all three points would be approximately conjunct one another and would signify a midpoint picture.

The tension suggested by the T-Square is quite pronounced, and this tension is inherent in the midpoint picture analysis. The three involved planets or points interact, pooling their respective characteristics in an attempt to reach the potential suggested by their interrelationship. By its nature, the T-Square represents considerable tension and is uncomfortable enough to prod us into action.

In Jim Henson's chart (figure 24), Saturn opposes Neptune, with both planets being squared by Jupiter. As we have learned, this aspect structure and the related midpoint picture could be interpreted as:

♃ = ♄/♆   *Rewards and recognition (♃) can be accomplished through giving substance (♄) to the dream (♆) or making the intangible (♆) tangible (♄).*

The T-Square represents the dynamic that we typically associate with midpoint pictures. Tension encourages us to take action. As we will see in the following pages, some special aspect structures differ in the nuance with which they influence the midpoint pictures.

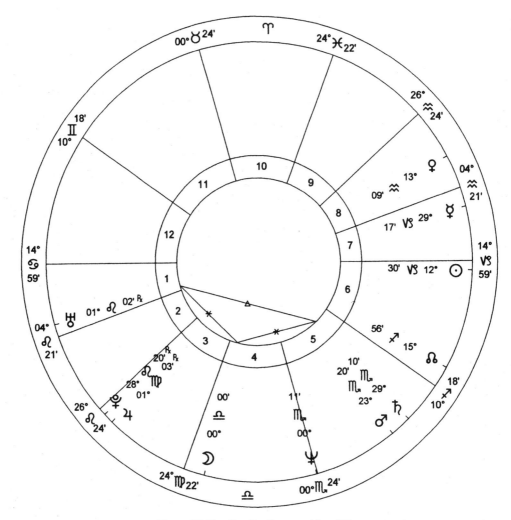

Figure 25. Two Sextiles Connected by a Trine

Mel Gibson
January 3, 1956 / Peekskill, NY / 4:45 PM EST
Placidus Houses

Two Sextiles Connected by a Trine

In charts where a Focal Point is connected to two sextiles, we may find a rather unusual arrangement in which the two planets or points that form sextiles[2] with the Focal Point are in a trine relationship with one another. This presents us with a somewhat contradictory situation. We have come to anticipate *tension* when we evaluate the impact of a midpoint picture. However, in this specific circumstance, we see the Focal Point and both of the planets or points in the associated midpoint all connected by quite harmonious and supportive aspects to one another.

Would it be reasonable to expect that this midpoint picture might have a relatively easy path toward making it all work together? Despite the inherent tension that we associate with any midpoint picture, this particular dynamic actually might be expected to transpire relatively smoothly.

In Mel Gibson's chart in figure 25, we find this special aspect structure. The Moon (which, incidentally, is also exactly at the Aries Point) is the Focal Point and is connected by sextiles to both Saturn and Uranus. We also see the trine connecting Saturn and Uranus. This structure represents a midpoint picture that could reasonably be interpreted as:

AP = ☽ = ♄/♅   *Potential for public projection* (AP) *and emotional fulfillment* (☽) *can be accomplished through breaking* (♅) *with tradition* (♄), *breaking new ground, breaking* (♅) *rules* (♄), *and bridging between traditional* (♄) *and innovative ways* (♅) *of doing things.*

Mel Gibson's range as an actor combined with his refusal to be typecast in certain roles have revealed an amazing versatility. His ability to connect with the public on an emotional level (Aries Point = ☽) through his acting roles is amplified by his willingness to explore more nontraditional roles and related pursuits, including his substantial skills as a director. Somewhat ironically—and backing up our theory—Gibson actually has gained public and professional stability (♄) by taking risks (♅). However, in July 2006, Gibson risked driving unsafely and was stopped for speeding and subsequently charged with DUI. His rule-breaking behavior and verbal outburst were widely publicized and provoked a very public (AP) emotional response (☽) to his actions and behavior.

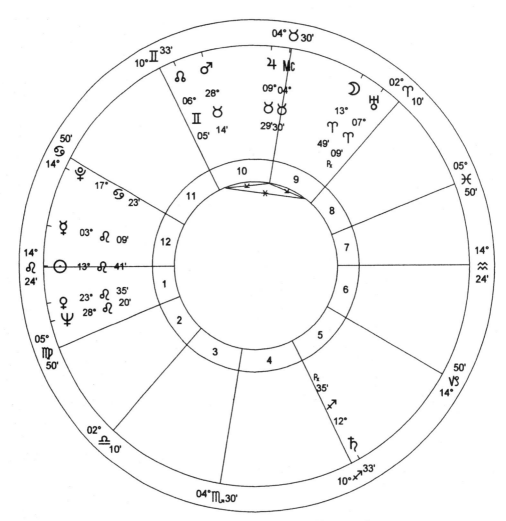

Figure 26. Two Semisextiles Connected by a Sextile

Andy Warhol
August 6, 1928 / Pittsburgh, PA / 6:30 AM EDT
Placidus Houses

Two Semisextiles Connected by a Sextile

Of the major aspects, the sextile arguably contributes the weakest influence. Keeping that in mind, the influence of the semisextile[3] is even weaker. When this book was in the early planning stages, I wouldn't have imagined making even a passing mention of the semisextile. But this special aspect structure merits consideration.

On first impression, this special aspect structure really doesn't seem all that special. In fact, it appears to be awfully boring and a probable underachiever. But when we recognize that this harmless-looking, decidedly unsexy combination of two semisextiles and a sextile also forms a midpoint picture, things get much more interesting. The reasoning goes something like this:

1. Midpoint pictures contribute tension.

2. Tension is uncomfortable.

3. If we are uncomfortable enough, we are motivated to change.

4. By changing, we can gain experience, grow, and evolve.

5. Soft or easy aspects (even relatively weak ones) could reasonably make the change/growth process go a little more smoothly.

6. Tension that potentially is more easily resolved justifies some serious attention.

The example in figure 26 shows Andy Warhol's chart, with two semisextiles from the Midheaven—one to the North Node and the other to Uranus. Uranus forms a sextile aspect with the North Node, so our special aspect structure is complete. The corresponding midpoint picture reasonably could be interpreted as:

Mc = ♅/☊   *Career pursuits and the public image* (Mc) *can be accomplished through an innovative* (♅) *relationship with the public* (☊), *or by public* (☊) *promotion of a revolutionary or unconventional* (♅) *viewpoint.*

Now that sounds like an awfully big deal for someone with the talent and aspiration to be an avant-garde artist, doesn't it? That is pretty impressive for such an apparently unassuming little aspect structure.

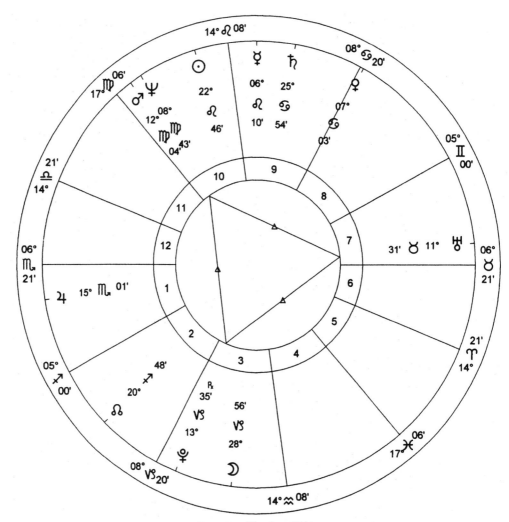

Figure 27. The Grand Trine

Napoleon Bonaparte
August 15, 1769 / Ajaccio, Corsica / 11:30 AM LMT
Placidus Houses

The Grand Trine

With the Grand Trine, there is a connection between three planets, with each one forming a trine to the other two. Although many of us have been led to believe that if we have a natal grand trine, then our lives will be charmed and we will meet our soul mate and win the lottery, the reality is often something altogether different. As delineated by Noel Tyl in *Synthesis & Counseling in Astrology*, the Grand Trine often suggests a self-defensive closed circuit of self-sufficiency that tends to isolate us. This attitude becomes so ingrained that one has to make great efforts to extricate oneself from this repetitive behavior.

Specifics of the Grand Trine dynamics are closely related to the element (fire, earth, air, or water) involved, but a detailed description of the interpretation of this aspect structure is beyond the scope of our current discussion.

Interestingly, the Grand Trine often also suggests powerful midpoint pictures. If the measurements are within a relatively tight orb, as in Napoleon Bonaparte's natal chart (figure 27), then three distinct midpoint pictures can be described. This fact helps us to explain the inherent tension in the Grand Trine. Even though the three planets or points are connected by the fairy godmother of the soft aspects (the trine), in reality the result can more closely resemble the intent of the wicked stepsisters. Isolation[4] may be strictly enforced and reinforced. One is rewarded (or at least not punished) for keeping to oneself and being self-sufficient. Self-isolation may represent a means of insulating oneself from sources of conflict or criticism. One may become so caught up in the repetitive nature of the Grand Trine that it is impossible to imagine any different frame of reference than what is represented by the status quo. Even if Prince Charming comes calling, the fear of leaving the predictable, controlled symbolic confines of the Grand Trine may result in a missed opportunity.

Napoleon's Grand Trine represents a synergistic interaction among Mars, Uranus, and Pluto that gives us three powerful midpoint pictures:

♂ = ♅/♇   *Efficient use of energy (♂) can be accomplished through innovatively (♅) promoting dramatic change (♇).*

♅ = ♂/♇   *Individualistic expression (♅) can be accomplished through energetically (♂) promoting dramatic change (♇).*

♇ = ♂/♅   *Sweeping dramatic change (♇) can be accomplished through aggressive (♂) rebellion (♅).*

Napoleon's Grand Trine and the associated midpoint pictures form a powerful combination of influences. As we discussed, the Grand Trine is often self-isolating. Priding himself on his militaristic prowess and trusting only his own judgment, he did manage to effectively isolate himself. But the tension suggested by Napoleon's midpoint pictures and the over-compensation to prove himself contributed to his short-term successes.

The Yod

This intriguing aspect structure is often referred to as "the finger of God." This interconnection links together three planets or points where the Focal Point forms quincunxes[5] with each of two other planets or points that are in a sextile relationship with one another. The quincunx suggests that *adjustments* are necessary to bring together disparate influences, while the sextile contributes an easy, free-flowing relationship. Combining these aspects into the Yod formation, we would expect the Focal Point to require adjustments with the two points connected by the sextile. However, the sextile should somewhat ameliorate the adjustment process because it connects the two points in the midpoint harmoniously.

For example, in Elvis Presley's chart (figure 28), we see this special aspect structure in which the Focal Point Saturn forms a quincunx with both Pluto and the Midheaven, with Pluto and the Midheaven connected by a sextile. This structure translates to the midpoint picture and the corresponding interpretation:

♄ = ♇/Mc   *Necessary controls, along with structure and stability (♄), can be accomplished through shaking things up (♇) publicly (Mc) or through desires to make dramatic changes and leave one's mark.*

In Elvis's chart, there is another example of this special aspect structure that is linked to the previous midpoint picture. Elvis's Midheaven also forms a quincunx with both Saturn and Uranus, with Saturn and Uranus connected by a sextile. This yields a midpoint picture that could be interpreted as:

Mc = ♄/♅   *Career pursuits and the public image (Mc) can be accomplished through breaking (♅) with tradition (♄) or by gaining stability (♄) through innovation (♅).*

Both of these special aspect structures suggest that the necessary adjustments (symbolized by the two quincunxes) can be achieved more easily by utilizing the harmonious connection (the connective sextile) to assist with the process. By utilizing the supportive energy suggested by the sextile in Elvis's break with tradition, the career adjustments necessary to bridge the chasm from tradition to innovation were eased considerably.

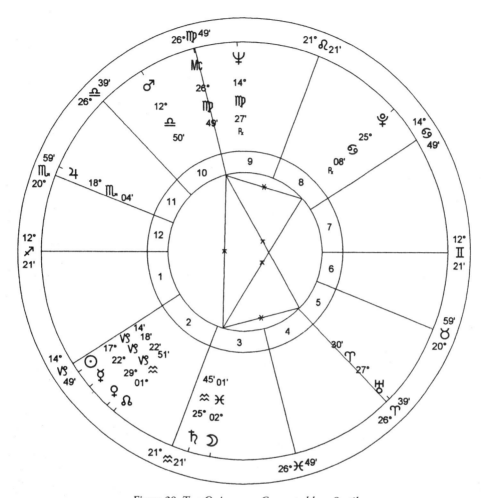

Figure 28. Two Quincunxes Connected by a Sextile

Elvis Presley
January 8, 1935 / Tupelo, MS / 4:35 AM CST
Placidus Houses

Two Quindeciles Connected by a Semisextile

The quindecile[6] (pronounced *quin-deh-chee'-leh*) is enjoying something of a revival, due in large part to the work of astrologers Noel Tyl and Ricki Reeves.[7] I generally look at the quindecile as a dynamic within the chart that cannot be ignored and must not repeatedly be swept under the carpet. If we're able to address the tension suggested by the quindecile, then great personal advances are possible. If not, it represents issues that will keep coming back until we finally recognize these influences and address them.

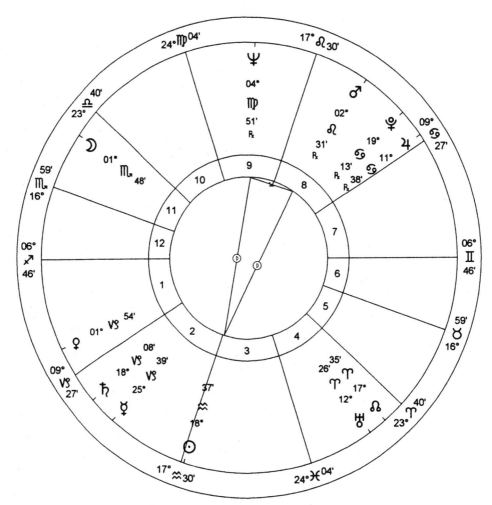

Figure 29. Two Quindeciles[8] Connected by a Semisextile

James Dean
February 8, 1931 / Marion, IN / 2:11 AM CST
Placidus Houses

In charts with a Focal Point linked to two quindeciles, we have a double whammy that amplifies the importance of addressing the compulsive nature of the quindecile. It is interesting to note that when this formation occurs, we also have a semisextile aspect between the other two points. While the semisextile is arguably one of the lesser aspects (even among the minor aspects), it does contribute a supportive influence and makes it somewhat easier to deal with the two challenging quindeciles.

In James Dean's chart (figure 29), we see that the Sun forms a quindecile aspect with both Mars and Neptune, with Mars and Neptune connected by a semisextile aspect. This describes a midpoint picture that could be interpreted as:

☉ = ♂/♆   *Ego needs and identity definition (☉) can be accomplished through use of charisma (♂/♆) or aggressively (♂) pursuing the dream (♆). (Note that Neptune is also associated with film/movies.)*

Dean's two quindeciles, by themselves, could have contributed an assertively self-centered focus (☉ ⓠ ♂) and a need for escapism (☉ ⓠ ♆). But with the supportive yet relatively weak semisextile, he was able to smooth some of the tension through use of his charisma (♂ ⊻ ♆).

This same formation also exists in Walt Disney's chart (figure 30), which involves four planets (due to the conjunction of Jupiter and Saturn), producing two separate but over-lapping midpoint pictures:

♆ = ♃/♅   *Imagination and inspiration (♆) can be accomplished through an unrestrained (♃) pursuit of individualistic expression (♅).*

♆ = ♄/♅   *Imagination and inspiration (♆) can be accomplished through bridging traditional (♄) and innovative (♅) methods or by breaking (♅) rules (♄). (Again note that Neptune is often associated with films/movies and fantasy).*

The combination of—and the contrast between—these two midpoint pictures contributes balance and diversity to their respective midpoint pictures. The Neptune Focal Point can be either inspirational or delusional. In the first, the semisextile (♃ ⊻ ♅) easily could go over the top with fantasy and have a difficult time grasping reality. In the second, however, the semisextile (♄ ⊻ ♅) contributes a welcome degree of caution that adds a measure of stability and structure.

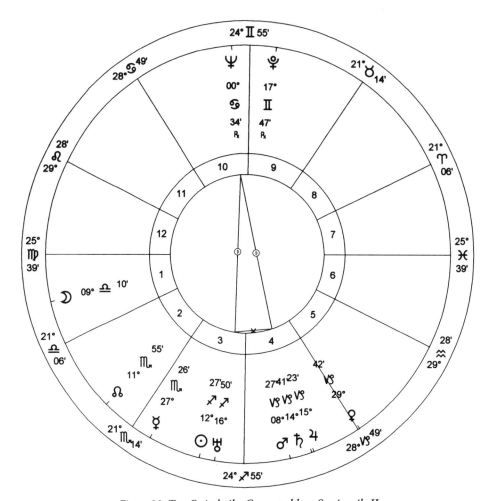

Figure 30. Two Quindeciles Connected by a Semisextile II

Walt Disney
December 5, 1901 / Chicago, IL / 12:35 AM CST
Placidus Houses

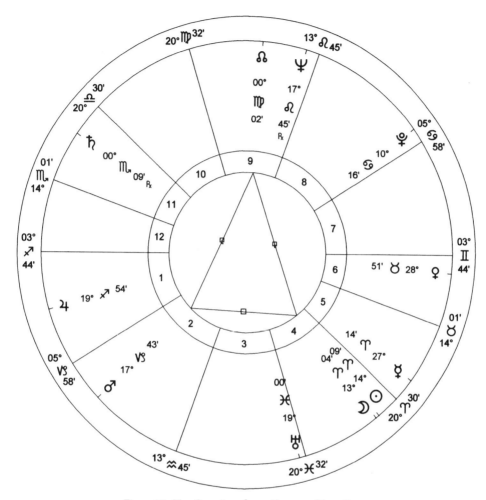

Figure 31. Two Sesquiquadrates Connected by a Square

Marlon Brando
April 3, 1924 / Omaha, NE / 11:00 PM CST
Placidus Houses

Two Sesquiquadrates Connected by a Square

When two sesquiquadrates[9] are connected to a single Focal Point, we once again take note of the inherent tension-inducing influence. While the sesquiquadrate contributes somewhat diminished squarelike tensions, it is fascinating to note that in this special aspect structure the two planets or points in sesquiquadrate aspect to the Focal Point also form a square aspect with one another.

Marlon Brando's chart (figure 31) represents two such cases, with some overlap between them because of the Sun-Moon conjunction. In the first case, the North Node forms a sesquiquadrate with both the Moon and Mars, with the Moon and Mars connected by a square aspect. In the second example from Brando's chart, the North Node forms a sesquiquadrate with both the Sun and Mars, with the Sun and Mars connected by a square aspect. These midpoint pictures and their corresponding interpretations are:

☊ = ☽/♂   *The relationship with the public (☊) can be accomplished through use of assertive drive or self-promotion (♂) to meet emotional needs (☽).*

☊ = ☉/♂   *The relationship with the public (☊) can be accomplished through a focused, passionate, relentless energy (♂) for ego definition (☉) and self-promotion.*

These midpoint pictures demonstrate Brando's volatile reputation—both on and off screen—even though the tension represented is somewhat less than that of a T-Square. Considering that Brando's Sun and Moon are both in Aries, we can understand some of the dynamic that led to his personal no-nonsense style that paralleled his role in *The Godfather.*

Two Semisquares Connected by a Square

When a chart has a Focal Point connected to two planets by a semisquare[10] aspect, with those two planets being linked by a square aspect, the arrangement suggests considerable tension and also describes a midpoint picture.

We see this configuration in John Belushi's chart (figure 32). There are semisquares from the Moon to both Jupiter and Neptune, with Jupiter and Neptune being connected by a square aspect. The midpoint picture and interpretation correlated with this configuration is:

☽ = ♃/♆   *Emotional needs (☽) can be met through expansive, unrestricted (♃) visions (♆), by believing (♃) in the dream (♆), or perhaps by excessive (♃) escapism (♆).*

The tension suggested in this midpoint picture is substantial, even though there are two minor aspects (the two semisquares) involved. While this midpoint picture identifies Belushi's expansive creativity, it also relates to the emotional need to escape, which was apparently a factor in his untimely death due to an unintentional drug overdose.

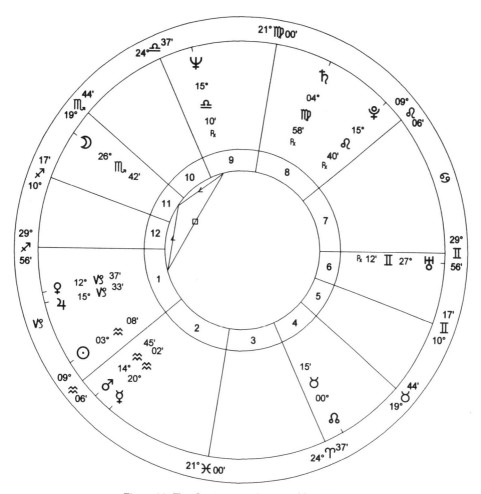

Figure 32. Two Semisquares Connected by a Square

John Belushi
January 23, 1949 / Chicago, IL / 5:12 AM CST
Placidus Houses

1. Note: In this section, a variation of Win*Star's "Novice" wheel is used for clarity in displaying the examples of special aspect structures.

2. The sextile (✱ = 60°) is a soft aspect that suggests a harmonious, supportive connection between the two planets or points.

3. The semisextile (⊻ = 30°) is a minor aspect suggesting a supportive influence.

4. Isolation may be of various types, including social, intellectual, etc., that can lead to the individual not being well integrated in his environment and with the people around him.

5. The quincunx (⊼ = 150°), also known as an *inconjunct*, is an aspect that suggests an *adjustment* that is necessary to integrate the two planets or points.

6. The quindecile (Ⓓ = 165°) is 15° on either side of an opposition, and is associated with obsession, compulsion, disruption, separation, and upheaval.

7. Reeves is the author of *The Quindecile: The Astrology & Psychology of Obsession* (St. Paul, MN: Llewellyn Publications, 2001).

8. In this wheel, the 165° quindecile aspect is signified by the glyph Ⓓ.

9. The sesquiquadrate (⚼ = 135°) symbolizes tension, but less than that of a square.

10. The semisquare (∠ = 45°) also represents tension, but less than that of a square.

Appendix I

90° Midpoint Sort and 90° Midpoint Tree Comparison

90° Midpoint Sort

Advantages

- Concise, compact, all-inclusive.
- This format is necessary to find Aries Point pictures and to locate the ☉/☽ or Asc/Mc midpoint.

Disadvantages

- Can be time-consuming to identify midpoints within orb of planets or points.
- Can be complicated when two or more planets or points share the same midpoint.
- Can be complicated to annotate when the Focal Point orb spans more than one column.
- Can suggest meaningless midpoint pictures within orb (such as ♂ = ♂/♆), in which the Focal Point is also included on the right-hand side of the equation.

90° Midpoint Tree

Advantages

- Groups midpoint pictures together by Focal Point and sorts them by closest orb.
- Lists only midpoint pictures that are *within the specified orb*.

Disadvantages

- Cannot identify Aries Point–related midpoint pictures.
- Cannot identify the ☉/☽ or Asc/Mc position unless they are within orb of a Focal Point.
- Midpoints corresponding to more than one Focal Point show up in multiple locations.
- Midpoints may not be listed in the standard order of fastest to slowest speed.

Appendix II

	Focal Point Keywords	*Midpoint Keywords*
☉	Life purpose and ego definition	Life energy, identity, ego, life purpose, illumination, authority figures
☽	Emotional fulfillment needs	Emotional connection, nurture, Mother, emotions
☿	Efficient thoughts and communication	Communication, the mind, diversity, ideas, quickness, eagerness, nervous system, movement, transportation, travel
♀	Social, aesthetic, or relationship needs	Social and relationship connections; anything *aesthetically pleasing* to the senses, such as art, music, food, love, marriage, beauty, and harmony
♂	Efficient use of energy	Applied energy, assertion, anger, aggression, drive, courage, impulse, force
♃	Optimism, expansion, or excess; rewards and recognition	Expansion, optimism, enthusiasm, excess, luck, rewards, religion, higher education and mind, internationalism
♄	Structure, stability, and *necessary* controls	*Necessary controls*, structure, stability, discipline, foundation, ambition, determination, rules, restrictions, restraint, repression, constriction, delays, tradition, authority figures, status quo, frustration
♅	Individualistic expression or innovation	Freedom, individuality, inventiveness, innovation; sudden unexpected change, rebellion, risk taking, eccentricity, avant-garde, rule breaking, nonconformity
♆	Sensitivity, inspiration, creative visualization, fantasy or escape needs	Confusion, idealism, camouflage, creative visualization; something other than it seems, spirituality, or inspiration, self-destruction, escape, drugs, alcohol, fantasy, fog
♇	Power needs; sweeping, dramatic change; empowerment, a new perspective, and transformation	Adds empowerment, perspective, and transformation; *power urges, necessary destruction before rebirth*, the phoenix principle, *symbolic death*; intensity; having a major impact

	Focal Point Keywords	*Midpoint Keywords*
Asc	Identity definition; personal projection	Outer expression of self; ability to connect with others; identity projection, personal expression
Mc	Career pursuits, profession, public image	Career pursuits, profession, public image
☊	Relationship with the public	Relationship with the public; making contacts, public exposure, working with others
AP	Potential for public projection	Potential for public projection

Appendix III

Natal Midpoint Analysis Interpretation Guidelines

The information contained within these guidelines incorporates symbolism suggested by specific astrological keywords. These keyword combinations can be used to create interpretive phrases and are intended to assist the reader in the development of his own interpretations.

When used in combination with the Focal Point keywords listed in appendix II, one can construct a meaningful interpretive sentence describing a particular midpoint picture (as described in chapter 2 of this book). The reader is encouraged to expand or revise these interpretations as deemed appropriate.

One should not expect all interpretive phrases to apply in every circumstance. More commonly, individual parts of an interpretation will be most applicable for a specific case. Each interpretation—whether positive or challenging—should be viewed as a possibility rather than a probability. Also, any individual may experience a wide range of the possible interpretations of a specific midpoint picture at different times in his life.

Guidelines for Use

Listings are presented beginning with the Sun and Moon, then proceeding planet by planet through Pluto and the North Node, and ending with the Ascendant/Midheaven. There is no difference in the interpretation of a ☿/♆ and a ♆/☿ midpoint. Rather than duplicate entries, interpretations are listed in the sections headed by the faster moving of the planets represented in the midpoint. Therefore, to find the listing for a Mercury/Neptune midpoint, one would first locate the "Mercury Midpoints" page and then scan down the page to find the ☿/♆ interpretation.

Sun Midpoints

☉/☽ An integration of emotional needs and ego needs to define life purpose

☉/☿ Illuminated or enlightened thoughts, ideas, and communication to define the ego

☉/♀ Illumination of aesthetics, social issues, or relationships; an ability to see the beauty; feelings of contentment

☉/♂ Utilization of relentless energy in pursuit of life purpose for ego definition and self-promotion

☉/♃ An expansive, optimistic approach to life with illuminated, enthusiastic goals and unlimited potential; confident pursuit of personal rewards and recognition; possible inflated ego, personal excesses, or self-aggrandizement

☉/♄ Ambitious, determined, and structured approach to ego fulfillment and life purpose; illuminated ambition; possibly a controlled or restrained ego

☉/♅ Illumination of individuality in an innovative or eccentric approach to life purpose; revolutionary spirit; possibly feeling above the rules

☉/♆ An illuminated sensitivity, imagination, dream, or spirituality; possible self-delusion or excessive need for escapism; possible ego or identity confusion or a unclear image of self

☉/♇ Powerful ego urges; self-assertion; compelling need to leave one's mark or make a big difference

☉/☊ An illuminated relationship with others; seeking out public attention, exposure, and popularity

☉/Asc An illuminated identity; self-confidence; self-discovery; possible self-centeredness

☉/Mc Defining ego through the career; seeking out public acclaim and exposure; thriving in the spotlight

Moon Midpoints

☽/☿   Meeting emotional needs through thoughts, ideas, and communication; communicating emotionally

☽/♀   Meeting emotional needs through social or artistic pursuits; emotional harmony; seeking idealistic perfection aesthetically or in relationships

☽/♂   Meeting emotional needs through assertive drive or self-promotion; possible emotional outbursts

☽/♃   Meeting emotional needs using optimism and expansion and being emotionally outgoing and demonstrative; unfettered emotions; emotional pursuit of rewards and recognition

☽/♄   Meeting emotional needs by use of discipline, ambition, structure, domination, or control; emotional responsibility and reliability; possible emotional reserve, restraint, or caution

☽/♅   Meeting emotional needs through innovative or eccentric means; embracing individuality; possible emotional detachment or volatility

☽/♆   Meeting emotional needs through idealism, imagination, dreams, or fantasy; emotional sensitivity, awareness; possible emotional confusion or deception

☽/♇   Intensity of emotions; needing to making a dramatic difference through use of emotions; emotional empowerment; perspective leading to transformation

☽/☊   Meeting emotional needs through maternal pursuits or by connecting emotionally with others; setting an example, being a role model

☽/Asc   Meeting emotional needs through definition of self; self-consciousness; emotional introspection

☽/Mc   Meeting emotional needs through career pursuits; a public display of emotions

Mercury Midpoints

☿/♀   Beautiful, harmonious, balanced communication, thoughts, and ideas; having a way with words

☿/♂   Energetic, assertive, or forceful thoughts, ideas, and communication; provocative, motivational, controversial, or argumentative communication; too many irons in the fire

☿/♃   Expansive, enthusiastic, optimistic thoughts, ideas, and communication; uncensored; open-minded; stretching the boundaries of the mind; possible tendency toward verbosity, to over-embellish or exaggerate

☿/♄   Giving structure or substance to thoughts or ideas by disciplined communication; creation of reality from thoughts, concepts, or ideas; controlled, organized thoughts; putting thoughts into a tangible form; possible oppressive or depressive thoughts

☿/♅   Innovative, unusual, unconventional, or even radical thoughts or ideas and communication; speaking unreservedly

☿/♆   Inspired thoughts, ideas, and communication of imaginative dreams or visions; fanciful ideas, communication; possible confused, distorted, or deceptive thoughts or communication

☿/♇   The power of words, thoughts, and ideas; communicating profound, deep concepts; persuasiveness; communicating a new perspective

☿/☊   Sharing thoughts, ideas, and communication easily with the public; a gifted communicator; a public spokesperson

☿/Asc Using thoughts, ideas, and communication to define self; an idea person; introspection; possible self-serving thoughts, ideas, or communication

☿/Mc   Communication in the career or through a public forum; public spokesperson

Venus Midpoints

♀/♂   Using energy for an aesthetic or social purpose; socially active; social activism; male-female awareness; sexual energy; intimate relationships

♀/♃   Expansive beauty, idealism, harmony, justice, fairness; social conviction or cause; possible overindulgence or excess; too much of a good thing

♀/♄   Making aesthetic beauty tangible; possible social caution or reserve

♀/♅   Unconventional, unique, or unusual aesthetic beauty; possible social unpredictability, unrest, or rebelliousness; not fitting in socially

♀/♆   Harmonious visions; a beautiful dream; idealism; possible social disorientation; confusion, delusion, or deception in relationships

♀/♇   Aesthetic or social transformation/new perspective; dramatic social change

♀/☊   Sharing or showing beauty or harmony to the public; pleasing, popular public image

♀/Asc   Personal aesthetic or social pursuits, being comfortable, at peace with oneself; appearance and image consciousness; self-awareness; putting best face forward; possible vanity

♀/Mc   Artistic or socially related career; social exposure or involvement; inviting public review; open to evaluation; a high-profile relationship

Mars Midpoints

♂/♃   Energetic optimism, expansion, confidence, growth, success; flamboyant; demanding respect; working for a cause; opinionated energy; over-the-top self-promotion; feeling unstoppable, invincible; "Damn the torpedoes, full speed ahead!"

♂/♄   Energetic drive to make progress; ambitious pursuit of a goal; fierce determination to conquer obstacles; possible energy use to control or dominate; frustrated energy

♂/♅   Energetic, relentless drive toward individualistic expression; innovative use of energy in nontraditional ways; possible impulsive actions or extreme volatility; a short fuse; heated outbursts; recklessness; risk taking

♂/♆   Charisma; energetically or aggressively promoting the dream or vision; being inspired to act or inspiring action in others; possible unclear or veiled motives or actions

♂/♇   Assertive power urges with energy used to promote or provoke meaningful change; lighting the fuse; assertive empowerment; promoting a new perspective; intense passion; possible intimidation or violent actions

♂/☊   Energetic interaction with the public; motivation; rallying the troops; inciting the crowd; possibly confrontational actions or behavior

♂/Asc   Energetic self-promotion, self-confidence or overconfidence; self-assertiveness, self-defensiveness

♂/Mc   Energetic pursuit of career; public self-promotion; a take-charge attitude; public assertiveness, leadership

Jupiter Midpoints

♃/♄   Cautious optimism; optimistic view of reality; overcoming limitations, obstacles, restrictions; pushing the limits; stretching the rules; extreme ups and downs

♃/♅   Expansive innovation and exploration; unrestrained individualistic expression; unapologetic, opinionated rebelliousness; possible recklessness or devil-may-care attitude

♃/♆   Expansive, unrestricted visions; believing in the dream; possible unrealistic optimism, delusions of grandeur, unclear goals, or excessive escapism

♃/♇   Strength of conviction and optimism for dramatic, sweeping change; expansive transformational change for growth; recognizing, embracing, or promoting necessary, inevitable change; potential for major recognition or financial rewards

♃/☊   Optimistic, expansive dealings with the public; an effusive public persona

♃/Asc   Trusting and showing off personal abilities and talents; self-confidence; seeking exposure to build confidence; can-do attitude; possible inflated ego

♃/Mc   Expansive career pursuits or public image; expecting public recognition or reward for accomplishment; possibly showing off publicly; benefits from public exposure

Saturn Midpoints

ħ/♅ Breaking rules; breaking with tradition; bridging old and new; gaining stability through innovation; bringing structure or organization to chaos; being an anchor in the storm

ħ/♆ Giving substance to the dream; making the intangible tangible; clarifying the nebulous; possibly losing touch with reality or having a clouded sense of reality; bending the rules; possible blurred or unclear boundaries, or deception to gain control

ħ/♇ Increased stability as a result of major change or sacrifice; meeting of irresistible force and immovable object; monumental power struggle between status quo and necessary, inevitable change

ħ/☊ Having a tangible, stabilizing, or controlling effect on the public; possible public caution or restraint

ħ/Asc Self-confidence; self-control; responsibility; maturity; self-discipline; possible cautious, reserved, or controlled identity

ħ/Mc Career determination, stability; building a career; controlled, reserved public image; needing to be in control, to be one's own boss; leadership; possibly a routine or boring job

Uranus Midpoints

♅/♆   Innovative or imaginative dreams or visions; eccentric fantasy; possible clouded or concealed individuality or eccentricity

♅/♇   Sudden, dramatic change for growth/rebirth; big changes for innovation; radical restructuring of perspective; possible disruptive upheaval

♅/☊   Innovative relationship with the public; public promotion of a revolutionary or an unconventional viewpoint; unusual acquaintances

♅/Asc   Being a free spirit and embracing individuality, eccentricity; an adventurer taking risks; nontraditional view of self; possibly having personal insecurities, feeling different, out of the mainstream, or like an outsider

♅/Mc   An unconventional or innovative career or an eccentric, unpredictable public image; public perception as an eccentric or a rebel; public expression of independence or uniqueness

Neptune Midpoints

Ψ/♀ Imagination and visions yield dramatic results; powerful yet hard-to-define concepts; the metaphysical; deception for power or dramatic change; sexual fantasy

Ψ/☊ Connection with the public using dreams or visions; a mysterious, chameleonlike public image; possibly deceiving or concealing something from the public

Ψ/Asc Visualization of self; possible unclear, inaccurate, or unrealistic view or portrayal of self

Ψ/Mc Spiritual or inspirational career or public image; visionary leader; unclear public image, concealed public behavior, or public deception

Pluto Midpoints

♇/☊   Having a major, dramatic, revolutionary impact on the public; publicly presenting a new perspective

♇/Asc   Self-empowerment, individual perspective, and transformation of self; powerful self-projection; revolutionary/evolutionary view of self; possible aloofness or self-dramatization

♇/Mc   Embracing empowerment, perspective, and transformation through the career or public image; shaking things up publicly; needing to make dramatic, sweeping changes; possibly craving power

North Node Midpoints

☊/Asc   Easy, intimate connection with the public; seeking public attention; definition of self through public lens; being comfortable with groups

☊/Mc   Working with the public in career; public image; increased visibility; high-profile image

Ascendant Midpoint

Asc/Mc   Identity awareness; melding of personal and public personas; fine line between personal and public identities; career defines identity

Appendix IV

Symbolic Manifestations of Unaspected Planets**

When a planet is unaspected, the individual must work particularly hard to...

☉	define the ego and determine the direction of his life pursuits. The challenge is in deciding where to focus one's energy.
☽	understand and pursue his emotional needs. The challenge is to find a way to integrate these emotional needs effectively with other personality traits.
☿	integrate his thoughts, ideas, and communication with his talents and his potential. The challenge is to be analytical and thorough without becoming obsessed with perfection, and to embrace diversity without becoming scattered and spreading oneself too thin.
♀	understand and integrate aesthetic and social needs into his life. The challenge is to find harmony and contentment in one's surroundings and relationships.
♂	find a productive and fulfilling outlet for his energy. The challenge is to find a constructive way to use this energy rather than gravitating toward impulsiveness or anger.
♃	find a productive outlet for his enthusiasm while avoiding the risk of excess. The challenge is to use optimism and strength of conviction in an expansive yet realistic pursuit.
♄	establish or adapt to necessary controls. The challenge is to maintain a balance between stability, structure, determination, and discipline on the one hand and inflexibility, stubbornness, and austerity on the other. All work and no play...
♅	feel comfortable with the expression of his individuality. The challenge is to find a constructive outlet for unconventional energies and to express—rather than suppress—individuality while avoiding any unnecessarily disruptive or even self-destructive paths.
♆	confidently pursue his dreams and visions while avoiding disorienting influences. The challenge is to channel creative energies positively instead of gravitating toward delusions or escapism.
♇	channel his intensity into an empowerment to make dramatic, sweeping changes. The challenge is to recognize that sacrifices often are necessary to allow continued growth and progress.

** This chart includes my own interpretations based on the information presented in Noel Tyl's *Synthesis & Counseling in Astrology*.

Appendix V

Midpoint Worksheet

AP = __/__ (88°00'–02°00' on 90° Midpoint Sort)	Potential for public projection; what we will potentially be remembered for	
Unaspected Planet(s)[1] (UP) 1) UP as Focal Point 2) Two UP in midpoint 3) One UP in midpoint	Gives analytical insight into UP interpretation; helps to integrate UP	1) 2) 3)
Focal Point = ☉/☽ (☉ & ☽ signs may be used)	Connects ego and emotional needs; forms the core of relationship dynamics	
Focal Point = Asc/Mc	Identity awareness; links personal and public focus; merging of internal and external	
Closest midpoint picture(s)	Often identifies a dominant theme in the individual horoscope	
Combinations of these planets in the midpoint:[2]	➤ **Suggest:**	
☽, ☿, ♀, or ♆	Idealism; aesthetics; creativity	
☉, ♂, ♄, or ♇	Power or control needs	
☿, ♂, ♃, or ♅	Impatience, restlessness, impulsiveness, recklessness	
☿ & ♄	Putting thoughts or ideas into a tangible form	
♂ & ♆	Charisma; inspiration to act	
♃ & ♄	Expansion vs. restraint; overcoming restrictions	
♄ & ♅	Old vs. new; control vs. freedom	

1. Unaspected planets (UP) make no major (Ptolemaic) aspects to another planet.

2. On the right-hand side of the midpoint picture equation.

Appendix VI

Midpoint Worksheet for Unknown Birth Times

AP = __/__ (88°00'–2°00' on 90° Midpoint Sort)	Potential for public projection; what we will potentially be remembered for	
Focal Point = ☉	Helps to define identity & personal projection in absence of a known Asc	
Unaspected Planet(s)[1] (UP) 1) UP as Focal Point 2) Two UP in midpoint 3) One UP in midpoint	Gives analytical insight into UP interpretation; helps to integrate UP	1) 2) 3)
Closest midpoint picture(s)	Often identifies a dominant theme in the individual horoscope	
Combinations of these planets in the midpoint:[2]	**Suggest:**	
☿, ♀, or ♆	Idealism; aesthetics; creativity	
☉, ♂, ♄, or ♇	Power or control needs	
☿, ♂, ♃, or ♅	Impatience, restlessness, impulsiveness, recklessness	
☿ & ♄	Putting thoughts or ideas into a tangible form	
♂ & ♆	Charisma; inspiration to act	
♃ & ♄	Expansion vs. restraint; overcoming restrictions	
♄ & ♅	Old vs. new; control vs. freedom	

Note: In cases of unknown birth times, we must exclude any pictures that include Asc, Mc, or ☽. The positions of the other planets and the North Node do not change enough in a 24-hour period to appreciably affect midpoint pictures.

1. Unaspected planets (UP) make no major (Ptolemaic) aspects to another planet.
2. On the right-hand side of the midpoint picture equation.

Bibliography

AstroDatabank Company. *AstroDatabank™ Software.* Manchester, MA. http://www.astro databank.com.

Bills, Rex. E. *The Rulership Book: A Directory of Astrological Correspondences.* Tempe, AZ: American Federation of Astrologers, 1971.

Ebertin, Reinhold. *The Combination of Stellar Influences.* Tempe, AZ: American Federation of Astrologers, 1972.

Hand, Robert. *Horoscope Symbols.* West Chester, PA: Whitford Press, 1981.

———. *Planets in Transit: Life Cycles for Living.* Atglen, PA: Whitford Press, 1976.

Matrix Software. *Win*Star Astrology Software.* Big Rapids, MI. http://www.astrologysoft ware.com.

Reeves, Ricki. *The Quindecile: The Astrology & Psychology of Obsession.* St. Paul, MN: Llewellyn Publications, 2001.

Tyl, Noel. *Solar Arcs: Astrology's Most Successful Predictive System.* St. Paul, MN: Llewellyn Publications, 2001.

———. *Synthesis & Counseling in Astrology: The Professional Manual.* St. Paul, MN: Llewellyn Publications, 1994.

Index

LLEWELLYN ORDERING INFORMATION

Order Online:

Visit our website at www.llewellyn.com, select your books, and order them on our secure server.

Order by Phone:

- Call toll-free within the U.S. at 1-877-NEW-WRLD (1-877-639-9753). Call toll-free within Canada at 1-866-NEW-WRLD (1-866-639-9753)
- We accept VISA, MasterCard, and American Express

Order by Mail:

Send the full price of your order (MN residents add 6.5% sales tax) in U.S. funds, plus postage & handling to:

Llewellyn Worldwide
2143 Wooddale Drive, Dept. 978-0-7387-0983-3
Woodbury, MN 55125-2989, U.S.A.

Postage & Handling:

Standard (U.S., Mexico, & Canada). If your order is:
$24.99 and under, add $3.00
$25.00 and over, FREE STANDARD SHIPPING

AK, HI, PR: $15.00 for one book plus $1.00 for each additional book.

International Orders (airmail only):
$16.00 for one book plus $3.00 for each additional book

Orders are processed within 2 business days.
Please allow for normal shipping time. Postage and handling rates subject to change.

Synthesis & Counseling in Astrology
The Professional Manual

NOEL TYL

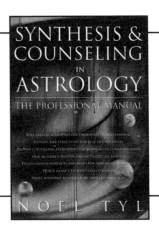

An astrologer's duty—to interpret and communicate what they see on a chart—is no easy task. They must make creative connections, know what to say when, and help their clients deal with life's most pressing issues.

Noel Tyl illustrates how astrological measurements—through creative synthesis—can be used to effectively counsel individuals. Concrete examples are provided through the horoscopes of 122 celebrities, historical figures, and private clients. Tyl also includes quick-glance transit tables and a natal and midpoint solar arc analysis directory.

1-56718-734-X, 912 pp., 7 x 10, charts   **$34.95**

Chiron

Healing Body & Soul

MARTIN LASS

Since Chiron's discovery forty years ago, astrologers have posed countless theories on the irrefutable impact of the "dark horse" planet. Going a step further, Martin Lass presents a groundbreaking new interpretation of the Chiron paradigm, demonstrating the comet's healing influence on present and past-life wounds.

From its mythology, birth, and discovery to its astrological impact, Lass offers a comprehensive understanding of Chiron and its place in the New Age movement. Highlighting its essential role in the horoscope, the author details Chiron's planetary characteristics: cycles, patterns, transits, and its influence in each of the signs, houses, and aspects. *Chiron* provides all the tools necessary to embark on a healing journey toward well-being and evolutionary consciousness.

0-7387-0717-1, 288 pp., 7½ x 9⅛   **$17.95**

Vocations
The New Midheaven Extension Process

NOEL TYL

People spend more of their lifetime working than doing anything else. A job is important not just for survival but also for a sense of personal fulfillment. Choosing the right vocation means having the ability to support yourself financially as well as gaining a sense of significance and success.

Seeing the vocation's profile within the horoscope has been one of the most difficult tasks astrologers encounter, burdened with laborious details. Now, for the first time ever, master astrologer Noel Tyl presents the "Midheaven Extension Process," a highly innovative approach to vocational astrology that is elegant in its simplicity and relevance to the modern job culture. *Vocations: The New Midheaven Extension Process* is a much-needed guide that will change forever the process for vocational consulting.

Noel Tyl (Arizona) is one of the foremost astrologers in the world. His twenty-nine textbooks have been teaching astrologers for two generations. He lectures in eighteen countries and maintains a worldwide client list of individuals and corporations. Tyl conducts his celebrated Master's Degree Certification Correspondence Course from his office in the Phoenix, Arizona, area.

0-7387-0778-3. 240 pp., 6 x 9 $17.95

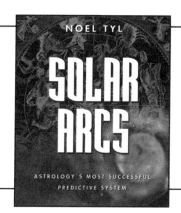

Solar Arcs
Astrology's Most Successful Predictive System

NOEL TYL

The first major treatise, in the history of astrology, on Solar Arcs.

Now available to all: Solar Arcs—the simplest of astrological prediction systems that harness the individualized symbolism of the Sun in the mechanics of future times. And with the computer, no more problems stand in the way of learning and applying Solar Arcs.

Noel Tyl, astrology's foremost analyst, writer, and teacher, presents the entire power potential of Solar Arcs with many case studies; he shows the work of Solar Arcs that is essential to authoritative rectification.

The book is also filled with bonus material: Tertiary Progressions, Rectification (with an exciting example using Sir Edmund Hillary), a 100-year quick-glance ephemeris, and Tyl's analytical synthesis of every one of the 1,130 possible Solar Arc and Solar Arc midpoint pictures.

- Author is a respected leader in the serious astrology market
- This master system of prediction is on the verge of decided prominence in usage throughout the astrological world. Tyl's lectures on the subject throughout 18 countries witness overflowing attendance
- Tailored for the advanced student and professional astrologer

ISBN 0-7387-0054-1, 480 pp., 7½ x 9⅛   **$19.95**

To order, call 1-877-NEW-WRLD
Prices subject to change without notice

The Sabian Symbols & Astrological Analysis

The Original Symbols Fully Revealed

BLAIN BOVEE

The Sabian symbols are a set of 360 channeled images corresponding to the degrees of the zodiac. A rich source of wisdom and inspiration, these symbols are indispensable for astrological analysis. *The Sabian Symbols & Astrological Analysis* offers an insightful look at the Sabian symbols, based on the original notations of their creator, Marc Edmund Jones.

Discussing each degree of the zodiac, Blain Bovee helps readers understand the Sabian symbols, while leaving plenty of room for individual interpretation. The extensive use of key words and phrases prompts the reader to use a creative approach and to find the relevance of a specific symbol to his or her life. Bovee also demonstrates how to draw meaning from astrological pairs and opposing degrees.

0-7387-0530-6, 312 pp., 7½ x 9⅛   **$19.95**

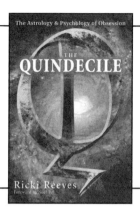

The Quindecile

The Astrology & Psychology of Obsession

RICKI REEVES
FOREWORD BY NOEL TYL

This book offers the first extensive analysis of the little-known astrological aspect called the quindecile (quin-deh-chee'-leh). Most astrology texts don't even address this 165-degree spatial relationship between planets that can point to obsessive-compulsive tendencies in the horoscope.

Most of us have some degree of obsessive-compulsive inclination wired into our instinctual databanks. Some are driven to be in a relationship, some need to prove themselves over and over again at work, and others continually eat or drink too much. When you come to understand the dynamics of obsession-compulsion tendencies as a human condition, you can enjoy a more balanced lifestyle as you learn to use this energy for benefit rather than as a hindrance.

Learn how to identify quindeciles in the chart, the dynamics of analysis, and how the aspect works when planets in one person's chart quindeciles those in another person's (synastry). Charts of celebrities are used as teaching tools, including those of Bill Clinton, Monica Lewinsky, Elvis Presley, and Mohandas Gandhi.

1-56718-562-2, 240 pp., 6 x 9   **$14.95**